MW01248444

POSITIONED TO PROSPER

A COLLABORATION TO ENCOURAGE BOLD MOVES

MANAGING EDITOR

Timeko Whitaker

a.i.c.
Authentic Identity Coaching

Positioned to Prosper
A Collaboration to Encourage Bold Moves
PUBLISHED BY
Authentic Identity Coaching, LLC
P.O. Box 36131
Indianapolis, IN 46236

www. Authenticinstitute.com
(317)710-9533

Please contact
Authentic Identity Coaching
For quantity discounts

ISBN: 978-0-9863401-3-0
Library of Congress Number: 2017912313
Printed in the United States of America

Editing & Book Layout by ASAP Writing Services
Cover Design by Studio 5 Agency
Photography by Xzibitz Portraits & Design

CONTENTS

ABOUT THE MANAGING EDITOR

For **Timeko L. Whitaker**, there is power in authenticity. She shares her life-changing philosophy with clients and audiences across the globe, empowering them to reach higher heights, embrace their core values, and achieve goals with her presentations and workshops designed to inspire, motivate and teach.

As a trainer, speaker, coach, author, and retired US military veteran, she is equipped to develop and train worldwide leaders and individuals alike, challenging all to live an authentic life of purpose. She is a certified John Maxwell Team Member, Speaker, Trainer and Coach, Founder and CEO of Authentic Identity Coaching, LLC and a certified Human Behavior Consultant specializing in (DISC) profiles.

Timeko has dedicated her business to helping all discover the power of authenticity. The guiding concepts of her mission are leadership, devotion, and servitude. Combining the keystones of military service, including Loyalty, Duty, Respect, Honor, Integrity, Selfless Service, and Personal Courage with key John Maxwell training principles, she shares wisdom and practical, applicable steps for those seeking personal and professional growth.

Through her company, Authentic Identify Institute, Timeko certifies others to become coaches and human behavior consultants.

After retiring from the U.S. Army in 2008, Timeko joined her husband, Eric Whitaker, in 10 years of Pastoral service, serving God through serving others. She holds a Bachelor's degree in Human Resource Management and a Master's Degree in Theology.

Timeko is the managing editor of *Hidden Identity* and a contributing author of *The Power of Mentorship* with notable authors including Zig Ziglar, Brian Tracy and others. She has coached both men and women to achieve their goals of becoming first time authors. Under her leadership, her publishing company has published over 60 first time authors.

Timeko serves as television host on TBN's WCLJ-TV's "Joy In Our Town" where she interviews community leaders, businesses, and organizations who are making a difference in our society.

While her goal is to help everyone, she encounters embrace their authenticity and significance, Timeko especially cherishes her role as wife to Eric and mother of two children; Daelin and Eyuana Whitaker.

Authentic Identity Coaching, LLC
P.O. Box 36131
Indianapolis, IN 46236
(317) 710-9533
authenticidentity@gmail.com
www.authenticinstitute.com
www.johnmaxwellgroup.com/timekowhitaker

INTRODUCTION

Jeremiah 29:11 *For I know the plans I have for you, declares the LORD, plans to prosper you and not to harm you, plans to give you hope and a future.*

As a Certified Christian Life Coach and the visionary for this project, I've been abundantly blessed with the opportunity to partner with some of God's most amazing people. You'll experience a few of them in this book. It is my pleasure and honor to present to you 11 passionate men and women of God who have answered the call to share their testimonies, encouragement, and love with the world.

Each author has come to an awareness that the significance of their past can aid in bringing others out of a place of pain and into a place of permission…Permission to move forward, permission to forgive, permission to believe and permission to prosper.

Our hope is that each chapter and testimony will ignite something deep on the inside of you that will give you strength and courage to maneuver past obstacles and to advance in life. We pray the words will emanate from each page to bring hope to every dead situation you may be facing. We pray that you will accept and believe that it is His will that you shall prosper.

Timeko Whitaker
Managing Editor

POSITIONED TO PROSPER

A COLLABORATION TO ENCOURAGE BOLD MOVES

Latricia Robinson-Dancer

Latricia Robinson-Dancer is a woman humbled by the presence of God in her life. She does not compromise when it comes to her relationship with God. Life has shaped her into a Worshipping Warrior.

She wears many hats in the Kingdom of God. She daily works out her soul salvation by encouraging those she meets. Latricia has served in the capacity of children's Sunday school teacher, pastoral care leadership, intercessory prayer, street ministry, mentorship ministry, and Jr. Usher coordinator. She formerly served as Armor Bearer to her previous First Lady in Michigan and evangelized as doors opened.

With a technical certificate in business administration with a specialty in management, Latricia has been an entrepreneur for over 20 years. She specializes in hair braiding and currently works at a pharmaceutical company.

Latricia thanks God for all of her family far and near. She is especially thankful for her wonderful husband, Robert, her four little angels; sons, Corey and Montrelle; daughters, Triniti and Traniece, who is now a mother. Latricia is thankful for her church family at Heartland Church in Indiana. Her favorite past times include worshipping God, shopping, watching movies with her family, playing her Nintendo, relaxing, and taking vacations.

"I have been crucified with Christ; it is no longer I who live, but Christ lives in me." Galatians 2:20.

CHAPTER ONE

My Life Restored

When Life Changed As I Once Knew It

When you are young, you think you have life by the horns. You throw caution to the wind and live life without thought of consequence. I was this way at 19. Engaged to be married, mother of a three-month-old, on top of the world ready to live life!

Then a visit to the doctor changed everything. I was diagnosed with cervical cancer. It is an understatement to say that I was scared. This was serious. I had to have surgery. I went into surgery feeling empty. There was a void in me that would not go away. At the time, I thought it was because I was sick and would leave once I was better. Not so.

Thinking back, this void was there before the diagnosis. I did not have a relationship with God. I did not go to church. I was shacking up and pretty much doing whatever I felt like doing. I had the surgery.

Afterwards my only thoughts were healing so I could be with my fiancée again. I was convinced this would fill that void; add substance to the emptiness I was feeling.

Two years later, wedding plans were moving along. I could hear wedding bells ringing all around me. The day of my bridal shower was finally here. Only six days to go and I would be a wife and mother! Finally, I would be fulfilled.

Not so!

My fiancée called off the wedding, took my car and left my son and me. Not only was my heartbroken but also the heart of my two-year old-son. We both wanted him back so badly. I felt hopeless. I was hurting. I was broken. I was overwhelmed with emptiness. I felt like that void in me was going to swallow me up.

Thank God for Mothers. His mom really encouraged me during this time. She gave me the wisdom I needed to get my life on track. She simply said, put no man before the Lord and everything will be ok. My mom then instructed me to go to church and let the Lord bless me.

I hadn't been to church in years. One week later, I went. Not really knowing why, I went up for prayer. The pastor started telling me I was tired of a lot and asked me if I wanted to be saved. I told him no, I'm not ready and went back to my seat.

Thank God for church mothers in Zion! A woman came and whispered in my ear. She began telling me all that I had gone through. She sounded like an angel. When she asked if I wanted to go back up and get saved, I said yes. As I stood there repeating the words that would save my life, I felt a chill; something lifted out of me. I never cried a tear but I knew change had taken place.

My journey towards God began that day. I began to learn about the power of the Holy Ghost. It was amazing. Three months into my journey, the day before Thanksgiving, God filled me with His awesome power. I received the Holy Ghost and my life has not been the same. That emptiness? That void? All gone! All filled with love, joy and peace. Yes, peace. I was able to forgive the man that left me and ask him to forgive me.

I have made many mistakes along the way with men being my biggest weakness. My life has changed dramatically. I just kept getting back up each time I fell, a little stronger than before. If you just hang in there, God will use the good, the bad, and the ugly to restore your life.

No eye has seen, no ear has heard, and no mind has imagined what God has prepared for those who love him. 1 Corinthians 2:9 NLT

The knock that would change my life forever

One day in 1998, there was a knock at my door. It was a guy I knew from school. I invited him in and we enjoyed good conversation. He left, but we kept in touch. I wasn't looking for a relationship. In fact, I was sick of men and tired of getting hurt. It's funny, but my first thought when I saw him was, no God not another man! Little did I know, God had a plan.

I have to say he intrigued me. He was different than other guys I had dated. I wasn't sure I was ready for a relationship. My emotions were fragmented and my self-esteem was shot. God used the book Beauty for Ashes by Joyce Meyer to make me whole again. I decided to give him a chance. I invited him to church to hear me speak and things progressed from there.

This man really seemed to love me. He had a genuine concern for me and my son. It was his treatment of my son that first drew me to him. He would tell me that I had metal walls up around my heart. I really wanted this to work, so I started lowering my walls. It wasn't long before I gave totally in and ended up in bed with him. I was immediately convicted. I fell to my knees right in front of him and cried out to God for forgiveness. I told God how sorry I was for letting him down. I'm sure this guy had never experienced anything like that before. When I got up, tears were running down his face. I thought, what did we just do?

One month later I found out I was pregnant with our middle son. I was so embarrassed. I thought my life was over.

One month later I found out I was pregnant with our middle son. I was so embarrassed. I thought my life was over. I tried to hide it from my church family. He had moved to Texas. I called and told him I was pregnant. He came back. He got saved. We got married. His family readily accepted my son and me.

My job transferred me to Texas. My pregnancy was high risk so I couldn't work. I was placed on bed rest. Away from family and friends, my husband was my earthly hero. He polished my toenails, gave me full body massages every other day all while working hard every day. He taught me a lot; he was a good provider, father, lover, and a jack of all trades. Our love was strong. We didn't have much materialistically but we had God and each other. My husband tried to please me in every way possible with all that was in him. My prayer was for him to please God the way he wanted to please me.

Fear not, you will no longer live in shame. Don't be afraid, there is no more disgrace for you. You will no longer remember the shame of your youth and the sorrows of widowhood. Isaiah 54:4 NLT

The call that would redirect our steps

The phone rang, "Hello, this is your step father (who has been God sent to our family) your mom has just been in a bad car accident."

Screaming and crying, trying to tell my husband what happened, all I could get out is we have to move back home. My mom is so dear to me. I had to be near her during her recovery process. My husband never argued. We moved back. My mother recovered.

Let's not forget, I'm still pregnant, but not for long. The contractions begin and I give birth to our son. Right after birth, his blood sugar dropped to 30 and the doctor could not get my uterus to tighten or stop me from bleeding. I only knew to call on the name of Jesus. I called, He answered. The doctors labeled it a miracle. Five years later, I gave birth to our daughter Triniti.

He sent His Word and healed them, snatching them from the door of death. Let them praise the Lord for His great love and for the wonderful things he has done for them. Psalm 107:20 NLT

Going through difficult times all at once

Life in Michigan was good. It had its challenges but our church family was awesome. I will always thank God for them. We were being given the opportunity to move to Indiana. We made the move not knowing what life had in store for us. Sometimes life comes at you so fast and fierce you don't have time to think. This is the way it happened when we came to Indiana.

The phone rings. It is my husband calling from work saying, "We have just been robbed at gun point! They held the gun to my head threatening my life and demanding I open the safe with just minutes to spare, it took three tries to open the faulty lock on the safe."

Three days before this, I was praying for him asking God to save his life. This incident changed the course of our life and my husband has never been the same, his personality has changed, he has secluded himself and lost all his joy.

A few years later, I was experiencing some type of illness. I finally went to the doctor. He announced, "You have to have surgery. If you can sign here we will get you scheduled."

I had been so sick I was ready for anything that would make me feel better. I had the surgery and God allowed it to be successful.

The following year I lost my beautiful grandmother who loved the Lord so. After that, another visit to the doctor with more tests. The doctor gives that gentle knock on the door and enters. She spoke, "According to the test results you have to have a major surgery." I quickly said no and left.

The days following were difficult because I knew I had to have this surgery. God helped me put on my big girl panties and go back. It was hard, but God saw me through. I wasn't popping back from this surgery as fast as I should have been. This was different. I just didn't feel good. My hair was coming out by the handful. I was having all kinds of symptoms. We called the doctor and he got me in within two hours. He immediately sent me to a specialist who cares for Lupus patients. I started a regimen of tests. One night I dreamed God healed me. When the test results came back it was a Vitamin D3 deficiency. To God be the glory.

I faced yet another health challenge. My mammogram came back abnormal; it was three cysts that had to be drained, which is a painful process. I am still enduring as these cysts grow back but I am trusting God for total healing.

It seemed as if this move to Indiana brought nothing but adversity to our lives. Just when I thought things could get no worse, my oldest son got into trouble at school. I have never had any trouble out of him. He was almost prevented from graduating the following year. God intervened. On the heels of this, I get a phone call from my doctor's office instructing me to immediately go to the emergency room and be admitted for emergency surgery.

Still healing from the surgery, my daughter suddenly became ill. The doctor told us to take her straight to the hospital. The results of her tests showed she had Type I Diabetes. Her blood sugar level was 642. My eight-year-old baby was on an insulin pump.

The next year was challenging. When she turned nine, I noticed a change in her demeanor. She was tired, depressed, and wanted to die. She was doing bad things to herself. She said voices were telling her to do these things. I called her doctor to rule out any issues with the medication.

My daughter said when she entered her room she felt something come over her. That's all I needed to hear. The devil is a LIAR! I began to war on my child's behalf through prayer, fasting, and confession of His Word. The devil was not paying any bills in my house and I served him an eviction notice. The fervent, effectual prayers of the saints were awesome. God gave the victory.

Our marriage was failing and only God could fix it. We still believe God to fully restore. There is nothing too difficult for him.

Later that year my mentor of sixteen years passed away at the age of 82. My husband was rushed to the hospital where he was in ICU for three days and almost died. God spared his life.

The next two years brought more loss. My good friend died of breast cancer. My precious daddy died. This really left my sister and I broken. All the heartache I had experienced in my life was nothing compared to this. I couldn't let him go. It was so hard. God said to me one day, you are letting a daddy go to embrace a Father like no other.

I am a Father to the fatherless. Psalm 68:5.

My marriage had taken a beating through all the adversity. My husband and I clashed on everything. There was no abuse, no cheating, we just lost sight of each other. So, it was no surprise when he announced he wanted a divorce.

I remember when we were best friends. We clung to each other through failing health and the issues of life arose. Now our love was seeping through my fingers like running water from a faucet. I did not see how to hold on to what we had, and I definitely could not grasp what was ahead. Our marriage was failing and only God could fix it. We still believe God to fully restore. There is nothing too difficult for him. Jeremiah 32:17

The righteous person faces many troubles, but the Lord comes to the rescue each time. Psalm 34:19

Standing Therefore

After being everything to everybody, the cares of life had beat me down. I was so exhausted and weak. I had no strength left to fight. I pleaded with God to take me out of this storm that was my life. God replied, no. If I take you out of the fire now you will be incomplete. Trust me, I'm there for you.

With tears streaming full of frustration I said, "God you can sock me in the eye, stomach, and back I'm not letting you go. I will not bow to Baal."

With that declaration, the fire intensified. My oldest son was in Utah. I got a call that he was hospitalized. His brain had shut down and he couldn't talk or walk. To make matters worse, because he was considered an adult, they would not tell me where my child was. He was hospitalized for 12 days. All we could do was fast and pray. They finally flew him home. He is now walking and talking and we believe God for total restoration: spirit, soul, and body.

I have struggled most of my life with what people thought of me. I am truly thankful to the support systems God had in place at each phase of my journey. I had lost many friends and was lonely. People just don't know what a person has gone through or is going through. They don't understand the hurt and pain or the reasoning behind why a person acts the way they do.

There was a season in my life where I didn't even like myself.

Bishop Walter Thomas said, "There's a moment when people can see your smile, but can't hear your scream"

I asked God, what are you doing? What are you trying to show me with these tests? God said, "We wrestle not against flesh and blood. You need to put on the whole armor of God and allow each test to be the building of your character for my kingdom." God said lay aside every weight and sin which doth so easily beset us.

I knew what stand meant but not to the extent in Ephesians 6:14 until I was living it. Some days I felt like I had cuts and bruises all over my body and someone with long finger nails poked every cut and watched me bleed, as I stood naked in a storm that was raining rubbing alcohol. Yes, it was an excruciating, painful time. I was in labor. I still had to push out the promises from God to get to my destiny. God was developing a Worshipping Warrior.

I had to ask God to forgive me. I was angry with him for not restoring and healing everything in my timing. I had to yield to the process. There are no short cuts to your destiny. I had to allow him to restore my confidence in Him.

Being confident of this very thing, that he which hath begun a good work in you will perform it until the day of Jesus Christ. Philippians 1:6

Being restored in the presence of God

I needed to be restored. Without any words, I fell to my knees. His presence was so real and powerful. I worshipped Him. His spirit was emerging with mine. All I had to do was to absorb His goodness.

Adversity, pain, heartache, and struggle have taught me the true meaning of worship. Nothing I went through or am currently experiencing is designed to destroy me. I realized all I had been through was now the wind beneath my wings. It was a tool in the hand of God so I could be Positioned to Prosper. My life has been restored by God's design.

What shall we then say to these things? If God be for us, who can be against us? Romans 8:31 KJV

Dear hearts don't give up on God because He won't give up on you. He's got you; you too CAN be restored by the presence of the Lord. To God be the glory, honor, and praise.

Endnotes:
Galatians 2:20
1Corinthians 2:9
Isaiah 55:4 NLT
Psalms 107:20 NLT
Psalms 68:5
Jeremiah 32:17
Psalms 34:19
Philippians 1:6
Romans 8:31

Ron Fudge

Ron Fudge is passionate about supporting the transformation of others, helping others to tap into their purpose, and utilizing his training and experience to yield positive results.

He is the owner and a lead consultant for Encompass Consulting Services, LLC, where he travels internationally transforming groups and individuals. He has extensive experience in working with urban youth and parents. He has served as a youth pastor, superintendent of Sunday school and business administrator for Greater Community Church of God in Christ in Benton Harbor, Michigan. In addition, he has served as the Benton Harbor Young Life director for youth ministry and a coordinator for community development for Council for World-Class Communities. He is a recent graduate of T. D. Jakes' School of Leadership through Regent University.

Ron has led the Volunteer Center of Southwest Michigan as the board president, while serving on a number of additional nonprofit boards in his local community. He is a certified diversity trainer, DISC trainer, and 5D Authentically Me Coach.

He has participated in numerous leadership academies and trainings through Lake Michigan College and Adaptive Schools, and has received extensive training in youth ministry through Young Life. Ron holds an accounting certificate from the Utica School of Commerce.

CHAPTER TWO

The Original Strategist

Abba

Pause for just a moment, and reflect on your children or someone you have cared for—whether you have mentored them, coached them, influenced them, or even had them live with you at some point. Now that you have this image in your mind, let us proceed. When the time comes that this person does well, folks begin to inquire about the people of influence in their lives. Imagine the feelings you get when someone you have impacted achieves a great accomplishment in life such as graduate with honors, start their own business, gets married for the right reasons, score the winning goal for a championship game, makes an extremely profitable financial decision, or simply takes out the time to value family members. Feels pretty good, doesn't it? All of the lunch hours, late conversations, loans, and mental energies invested have paid off. These are the kinds of returns you have prayed and longed for since the initial deposit in the mentee. So! With that being said, lets dine on the thoughts about what our Creator's, or Heavenly Father's thoughts might be about the total wellness and prosperity of His children.

Since the original craftsmanship of mankind, the Creator sustains His creation upon His shoulders. Genesis gives us the Garden, the woman, and the foundation of the existence of the cosmos. Psalms provides layers of encouragement. Proverbs make us look like geniuses as we follow and submit to the woman called Wisdom. Yes, wisdom is referred to as a her. The book of Malachi informs us how to keep a flow of supernatural wealth accessible to us (Malachi 3:10 KJV). The four gospels bring everything into right alignment as it relates to the well-being of the total man. The intentions of God's provision for His people and non-believers are clearly embedded throughout the book of life, but I will hang my hat on the ones I have mentioned for now. However, I will get to the heart of the matter later...

Set Up For Success - The Umbrella Table

Allow me to share a balcony view of a story about a strategically placed umbrella table in a quiet neighborhood near Grand Rapids, Michigan. It all happened on June 14, 2017. I was making myself comfortable at one of my "offices"—let's just call this particular "office" the Coffee Shop. This is one of my favorite places to spend time generating the "new" and "the what's to come" in my life. It is one of the places I go when I need to just be still and hear. As I sat down with my cup of coffee, computer, and notebook, there it was— something peculiar caught my eye.

There was a bold, uniquely sized lady who chose to journey outside in a black nightgown. To her defense, that day was hotter than a forgotten skillet on the stove.

She proceeded to the backyard, and pulled a table frame from behind a wooden fence. I'm thinking to myself, What kind of country girl shenanigans is this sister up to across the street? She carefully constructed this umbrella table at the corner in front of her home. From my view, I couldn't see the entire scene play out. So, I decided to mind my own business. Suddenly, a teenage man appeared. Come to find out, the umbrella table was designed for the young man. Then it dawned on me that this was not just "some country girl shenanigans" after all. This uniquely built, nightgown-wearing mom had actually positioned her son to prosper right in the front yard of their home. Considering it was extremely hot that day, this young man simply decided to set up a business. He was selling lemonade to folks walking and driving by his house.

Some of us have been blessed to be the recipients of intentionality from folks that were placed in our now—who had the ability to see into our future.

You may wonder how this qualifies as a "position to prosper" moment? I'm glad you asked. Let's start with the fact that he is working as a young man—so he is already developing a strong work ethic. He is also making a profit for the services he's rendering. Boldness is displayed as he engages with strangers, asking them to purchase his product. It also shows that he has a sense for when an opportunity exists because he provided a product that was perfect for the current conditions of his community (It was hot!). He capitalized on the conditions, and seized the moment to prosper. Some by-standers simply donated to his cause because of his effort to be in a position to prosper.

This moment should cause us to reflect on moments, events, or people that have had some kind of influence on our lives as it relates to our current position to prosper. Some of us have been blessed to be the recipients of intentionality from folks that were placed in our now—who had the ability to see into our future. Those who made a conscious choice to leave us better than they found us. As you reflect on these individuals, I'm hoping you become so overwhelmed with gratitude that you reach out to them or continue to allow them to live through you as you pass on the principles to the next generation.

"Prosperity is a way of living and thinking, and not just money or things. Poverty is a way of living and thinking, and not just a lack of money or things." Eric Butterworth

The Stewardship Factor

Let's dive into the life of another young man who went off to college and studied accounting. After completing an accounting certificate program, he went on to work for the Bank of New York. This was a great accomplishment, considering his prior educational and life challenges. Due to life circumstances, he decided to go back to his hometown. This meant packing up, leaving the job, and heading back across the country. As he re-established himself in his hometown, he began to thrive again in the banking industry. As he begins to understand the credit world and recognizes the advantages he had as a banker, he began to indulge in debt. Unfortunately, he had no prior experience with debt management. Whenever the ability to manage what you possess eludes you, its abuse is inevitable. This wonderful feeling of finally having the ability to get whatever he wanted, for a once financially wealth-deprived young man, was extremely appealing. Yet, it was disastrous. He did not understand the long-term value of living within his means and consistently paying his bills in a timely manner. He didn't realize how essential these things were to the health of his future prosperity. Needless to say, a slippery slope toward debt and all that comes with that was the outcome based on the lack of knowledge and experience. Multiple bankruptcies accompanied his life. So, what was once a beautiful place of prosperity swiftly became a bitter place of regret. He began to pray preposterous prayers like, "God, please disturb the bank computer systems to reflect that I'm debt free."

Well! God eventually helped him erase the debt, but not without some father to son chastisement about managing what he receives with integrity. So—no, the whole "Puff the magic dragon" computer system scam request of God did not take wings. It actually goes against a well-known principle established by God called, "reaping and sowing". He was entitled to the heartaches he reaped by the sequence of unprosperous choices he had made. Rethinking his request of God, he decided to ask a different way. The revised request goes as such, "God, if you help me re-establish my ability to prosper financially, I will take care of any stewardship opportunity you allow me to encounter."

The Creator must have been extremely pleased with his second approach because the young man has been completely and abundantly restored. He has kept his word about managing well his prosperous moments, which qualifies him to enjoy continual upgrades in the prosperity category. His current state has no resemblance of his past, which reminds me of 2 Corinthians 5:17 which states, *If any person lives for Christ, his old personality has vanished and a new way of being has emerged.*

So, maybe at this point being "positioned to prosper" has little to do with God's next move, but all to do with how we handle what we already possess. I'm convinced that when Christ announced, "It is finished," that it included our ability to prosper. If this is true, and it is—I would like to offer further encouragement to this young man and you as the reader. God has provided boatloads of principles which are married to promises. So, continue to follow the principles of the Kingdom—so your access to the King remains in motion like a flowing river.

Oh! There is one more thing I must say about this young man. He reminds me so much of myself. I felt like I was writing about my own journey. Was I? Maybe so! Stay tuned for now. I'm choosing to pause on this matter.

"Failure is an absolute prerequisite for success. You learn to succeed from failing." Brian Tracy

Faith = Access

Ponder upon the times when you were locked out or you locked yourself out of a place, relationship, opportunity, or experience that you once enjoyed the luxuries of attracting benefits or privileges. If these events have not occurred in your life then we need to talk, because I want to know your secret to pulling off such a feat. However, I'm certain each us can extrapolate some moment in life where we could have made better decisions about the opportunities that have slipped through our hands. As we reflect, lets also think about what could have been derived from the reversal of such mishandling.

My children and I walk out this scenario on multiple levels. We live a principle-driven relationship because, as a father, it is my role to pass onto them values and beliefs that are tried and proven in my life. These values and beliefs are transferable to the next generation, and they can cause a continual flow of blessings in one's family for eternity. For example, when my children want to borrow money from me, this allows me to ask questions that they must answer because they're in a place of need. Questions such as: How will you be using the money? When and how will you pay me back? I will proceed further by informing them that I expect full payment of the agreed amount; and if the agreement is not fulfilled, it will affect their ability to have access to like privileges in the future.

Well, you can image that this method calls for a plethora of patience and love. And, yes, debt cancellation plans and do-overs are back pocket strategies that a good parent chooses when necessary or desired. Some children catch on faster than others, so this causes for a greater application of wisdom on my part to govern these relationships with tailor-made care, while yet operating in principles that will still get the desired outcome— which is to expose them to the world of benefits by keeping your word and following through.

Faith in the Kingdom of God can be viewed in such a way as well. Faith is the vehicle we use to extract the possibilities of a heavenly partnership. As a matter of fact, it is the only way to have full advantage of such divine partnership and benefits. When we engage with our Heavenly Father, He demands FAITH be the key to our course of engagement. Knowing that God is a Spirit, it requires faith, because we can't see him unless He decides to reveal Himself to us in some form. However, he will still require us to journey with Him in faith and by faith. And without faith, it is impossible to please him.

For whoever would draw near to God, must believe that He exists and that He rewards those who seek Him. (Hebrew 11:6)

I'm delighted, with joy and boldness, to inform you that at this point my life is a lively example of being in a "position to prosper" by this Faith key.

Consider this viewpoint. Most janitors usually have keys to every door in whatever business or organization that has entrusted them with such an opportunity. These individuals are usually people who have already proven themselves to be trustworthy of such position, or someone simply decided to hook them up based on relationship or some other unique circumstance. Nevertheless, once the position is accepted by the benefactor, the power one possesses at that moment must be understood and valued—or this moment will be short lived. The control of the environment lies in the hands of one such individual; the ability to help others access their respective places; the going and coming of day-to-day business transactions, the maintaining of the mission of such a facility all comes with the ownership of such position.

Kingdom citizens have even more privileges with this key called FAITH since this position allows you the ability to extract whatever you need from God's place of provision for yourself and those connected to you. It allows you an advantage over those who choose not to use the key. Innovation and creativity loves to be unlocked by this key. Impossible feats jump for joy in heaven when this key is placed in the lock, just like a pet jumping for joy as its master returns home. Generations can be framed and stabilized by the effective use of such a key. The beauty of obtaining such a key is that it is accessible to whomever chooses to partner with the owner of such an organization called the Kingdom of God.

I'm delighted, with joy and boldness, to inform you that at this point my life is a lively example of being in a "position to prosper" by this Faith key. The use of this key happens 24/7 in my life, and I'm pleasantly ok with that reality. Exposure to the key of faith has come through some awesome mentors like Bishop Nathaniel Wyoming Wells Jr., Pastor Joique Bell Sr, Dr. Jerome Glenn and Betty Fudge-Fisher. These individuals have modeled this faith principle before me that has left a lasting impression on me for life, and my greatest respect for them comes in the form of continuing to exercise this principle in my life and passing it on to my children.

For whatever I lack according to the standards of others, my faith supersedes the differences. When others say I can't do something, I don't waste my time arguing with them. I allow them to have a growing moment in life, on my tab, as they watch me accomplish what they perceived could not happen because of my human frailties. This is true, but it's not from my human frailties that I operate, it is by the faith in the Word of God that anchors my way of being and my prosperity.

So, since this has proven to be a strong propelling truth over all the years of my life, why should I abandon what continues to work for me whenever I'm in POSITION to use this key. As a matter of fact, take that same Faith key out of your pocket, and pursue every dream, vision, idea, innovative invention, family goals, career goals you have had and show the world what it looks like to be a child of the King or to be a Kingdom Citizen. Just in case they, or you. want to know how you can have this authority to accomplish such extraordinary events. It's simple! God, through Jesus Christ, promised and delivered authorization.

The thief comes only in order to steal and kill and destroy. I came that they may have and enjoy life, and have it in abundance [to the full, till it overflows] John 10:10 AMP

Jesus looked at them and said, "With man this is impossible, but with God all things are possible." Matthew 19:26 NIV

I was that debt-stricken young man—and look at me now! Thriving and prospering!

If the previous content is not enough to convince you, just continue to watch my life as I enjoy the easiness of life because of the provision of the Heavenly Father as he STRATEGICALLY POSITIONS ME TO PROSPER.

Here I go!

"The strongest single factor in prosperity consciousness is self-esteem: believing you deserve it, believing you will get it." (Jerry Gillies)

He will be like a tree firmly planted by streams of water, which yields its fruit in its season, and its leaf does not wither, and in whatever he does, he prospers.
Psalm 1:3

Monica Sanders-Gates

Monica Sanders-Gates is excited to see what the future holds creatively and spiritually. Although Monica has worked as a respiratory therapist for the past 25 years, her first love is fashion and design.

She is a self- taught seamstress and has been sewing since the age of twelve. She enjoys redesigning clothes as well as creating some of her own designs through her company Designs by Mo Mo. Some of her favorite creations have been praise dance outfits, mime robes, and costumes for holiday productions at her church, New Horizons Outreach Ministry in South Bend, Indiana.

Monica was raised in Waterloo, Iowa and moved to Rock Island, Illinois as a teen. She graduated from Rock Island High School in 1981. She relocated to Dallas, Texas soon after high school. She graduated from El Centro College as a respiratory therapist in 1992. She has a Bachelor Degree in Theology from New Horizons Bible College and is currently attending Bethel College working on her Bachelor in Business. Monica is the wife of a loving and devoted husband, Terry Gates, and mother of a beautiful and talented daughter, Morgan. They reside in Granger, Indiana.

CHAPTER THREE

God Said Live!

It was just another typical hot July day in Texas. I had started the day with my usual morning routine. The sound of the can opener sent my two cats scrambling to the kitchen for their daily dose of Fancy Feast. My husband and I both worked as respiratory therapists. He worked the night shift at the local hospital and I worked days at a long-term care facility. He was just getting home as I was rushing out the door to fight the morning traffic. On the drive to work that morning, I couldn't shake this uneasy feeling. Something just wasn't right. I was very down that day. I felt a sadness that I had never felt before. I couldn't quite figure out what was wrong. On the outside looking in, people would say that I had a great life. My husband loved me. He gave me anything I wanted. We were both earning a good salary. I just wasn't fulfilled. I didn't want to live anymore.

I had been through back surgery and still had a full bottle of muscle relaxers. I decided that this would be my last day at that job, in that marriage, on this earth!

That evening when I got home, I fixed myself an ice-cold glass of Coke and retreated to my bedroom where I proceeded to swallow three or four pills at a time until the bottle was empty. My husband was in the shower getting ready for his 12-hour night shift. By the time he had finished showering and emerged from the bathroom dressed in his scrubs, I was already drowsy. He couldn't understand why I was napping at six o'clock in the evening. He went about his pre-work routine of coffee, fixing his dinner, and watching the evening news.

When he came in to kiss me goodbye, he sensed that something was not right. I had carefully placed the empty medication bottle under my pillow, out of sight. But my husband was trained to recognize the signs of an overdose. He kept asking me if I had taken anything. I finally admitted what I had done and he was able to drag my limp body to the car. I was in and out of consciousness on the way to the hospital. God had a plan for my life. I wanted to die that day, but God said live!

For I know the plans I have for you, declares the LORD, plans to prosper you and not to harm you, to give you hope and a future (Jeremiah 29:11 NIV)

Still Here

When I finally woke up in the ICU at the hospital where my husband worked, it was two days later. I remember being very angry that I was still alive. What had gone wrong? How was it possible that those pills didn't take me out? Then it all came back to me. My husband had driven me to the emergency room and let me out while he parked the car. I passed out on the ground before I even reached the automatic doors. I vaguely remember being loaded onto a gurney and rushed into a room.

They kept me for a few more days and then sent me directly to Charter Hospital for psychiatric evaluation and treatment. I was sad and angry at the same time. I did not want any treatment. In the state of mind that I was in, I could not see a light at the end of the tunnel. I just wanted to end my miserable existence. After they got me all checked in, they allowed me to go to my room and rest before dinner. I wouldn't see a doctor until the next day, so I was stuck there for at least one night. Tomorrow the doctor would tell them that I'm not crazy and let me go home.

The longer I sat there in that cold, dark, dreary room, the more I thought of ways I could end it. As soon as it came to me, I quickly went into the bathroom and made a noose out of the shower curtain. I was a mere 125 pounds at that time. I put my neck in the noose and bent my knees so that my feet were off the floor. The industrial strength curtain and hooks held me for quite a while. I felt myself passing out and then I was falling through a dark tunnel. It was the scariest thing I had ever experienced. I just kept falling. It was like it was never going to end. I thought to myself, this *must be what Hell is like.* I wanted desperately to turn around and come back, but I just fell deeper into the dark abyss. All of a sudden, I woke up on the cold bathroom floor with a terrible headache. The curtain had broken and I had fallen and hit my head on the floor. Scared out of my mind, I jumped up and ran as fast as I could down the hall to the nurse's station. I must have looked like a mad woman sprinting down that hall. The nurse demanded to know what kind of drugs I had taken. I confessed to what I had done and she immediately sentenced me to suicide watch. I was confined to a mattress on the floor with no covers and a camera detecting my every move until the doctor could see me the next morning.

Dawn of a New Day

The next morning, I was first on the list to be seen. Meeting with him was a pleasant surprise. He was very personable, kind, and compassionate. He seemed to know the pain I was feeling and exactly what was needed to pull me out of my deep depression. He prescribed an antidepressant, group therapy, and one-on-one counseling.

I was fortunate enough to have a husband who didn't complain about having to take care of all the financial responsibilities at home while I recuperated in the hospital. I was there for about two weeks and developed a whole new outlook on life. I was feeling so much better and looked forward to getting out and getting back to life as I once knew it.

My husband welcomed me home and we decided that I would not go back to work for a while. I continued with outpatient therapy and my antidepressant medication. I was starting to feel better than I had ever felt. My therapist said that the medication would help to elevate my mood, but that it would be good to talk about why I was so sad. She took me all the way back to my childhood. With her probing questions, so many unpleasant memories came flooding back to me.

Ugly Duckling

My first experience with embarrassment and shame happened when I was about four years old. My sisters and I were singing for my mother and some of her friends on the sidewalk outside our house. She and the other ladies were on the front porch clapping their hands as we sang "Oh happy day, Oh happy day." The next-door neighbor was also on her front porch with a friend of hers. I saw her out of the corner of my eye, pointing at me and saying something to her friend. It sounded like she said, "That black one." I don't know what she said after that but I know that I didn't like the feeling I got. We were all black. What was she talking about?

I began to examine my skin tone and noticed that I was darker than my two sisters. I developed low self- esteem from that point on; constantly comparing myself to others. I never felt like I measured up. I felt ugly next to my oldest sister. She was pretty, smart, light-skinned, and a cheerleader! Everything I was not.

For I know the plans I have for you, declares the LORD, plans to prosper you and not to harm you, to give you hope and a future

My life went a lot like the story of the ugly duckling who never felt like he fit in. He was teased and ridiculed by everyone and felt like he was not as attractive as his siblings. Not only did I feel ugly, I kept very quiet. I was paralyzed with fear if I had to speak in a room of more than two people. Consequently, I did not make friends easily.

The therapy session brought up so many of the negative experiences I had while I was growing up. When I was in junior high, I only had two friends. One day when I went to join them in the cafeteria for lunch they were already seated. As soon as I sat down, they got up and left. I was so humiliated and hurt. That seemed to be the story of my life. No one wanted to be bothered with me.

In high school, I was kicked out of a class for being too shy. I was taking a health occupations class that allowed the students to train as nursing assistants. We did clinical training in the hospital and the local nursing home.

After we had completed enough hours, we were able to work in the hospital or nursing home after school. One day the teacher called me into the hall and told me that I was no longer allowed to come to her class. She said that since I was so shy she didn't think that I was cut out for a career in healthcare. She said I would be better suited to a job cleaning floors because I would not have to interact with people. I was crushed; another blow to my self- esteem.

Making Progress

After months of intensive therapy, I was finally able to go back to work and live a somewhat normal life. I continued taking the antidepressant and visiting my therapist once a month. My husband and I decided that a change of scenery would do us both good, so we signed on with a company for travelling respiratory therapists. Every three months, the company would transfer us to a different state where we would work in the hospital. They put us up in fully furnished luxury apartments. We went to Maryland, Illinois, Texas, Nevada, Kansas, Pennsylvania, and Virginia. After a couple years of travelling, we decided to settle down in Atlanta. We purchased a home soon after we arrived and life was good.

Fast Forward

Years later, I found myself a single mother of a beautiful baby girl. Her father wanted nothing to do with either of us. I was out of work and practically homeless. Jackie, a dear friend of mine, invited us to stay with her while I looked for work. Since I had no job, I had no insurance, therefore, I would not be able to refill my prescription for antidepressants after my supply ran out. I was starting to panic. What if I got depressed and suicidal again? I was so afraid that I was going to leave that precious little girl without a mother.

Jackie invited me to church the Sunday after we arrived. I hadn't set foot in a church in years. I didn't have anything to wear, so she let me borrow a dress. I really enjoyed the service and looked forward to the next time. I went to Wednesday night Bible study and then back again on Sunday. About the third Sunday I went down for the altar call. I was ready to accept Jesus as my Lord and Savior.

That was the best decision I ever made. I couldn't believe how good I felt. I just couldn't get enough of Jesus. All I wanted to do was read my Bible and any literature that would help me to get to know Him. The TV in my room was tuned to TBN every minute of the day. I was on fire for God! Soon after, I was baptized and I also dedicated my baby girl back to the Lord.

I was blessed to receive the maximum amount of unemployment allowed because of the good salary I earned when I was working. It wasn't long before I found work and was able to afford my own place. My newfound relationship with the Lord allowed me to see His hand in my life. I don't even recall exactly when He delivered me from depression and suicidal thoughts.

Months after I had run out of my antidepressant medication it occurred to me that I didn't have that sad gloomy feeling that had plagued me most of my life. It had been replaced with joy.

For His anger is but for a moment, His favor is for life; Weeping may endure for a night, But joy comes in the morning. (Psalm 3:5 NKJV).

The Joy of the Lord is My Strength

It has been 13 years since I took my last antidepressant. I had been diagnosed with depression in the early 90's and was on medication to treat it for about 12 years. I believe it is a miracle that I was able to abruptly stop taking medication for that condition without any negative side effects. I wouldn't advise anyone to go off of their medication without first consulting their physician. I did it because I had no choice. It worked out in my favor because it was a part of God's plan. He knew that I was going be out of work with no way to afford my medicine. I would have to turn to Him.

I praise you because I am fearfully and wonderfully made; your works are wonderful, I know that full well.

When I look back over my life, I see how God has been with me. The two suicide attempts that I referenced in this story were not the only ones. Each time God spared my life because it was not His plan for me to leave this earth right then. He has a strategic plan for everyone's life. The experiences in our lives, whether good or bad, help us to become who God created us to be. He has positioned each and every one of us strategically. Like chess pieces on a game board, everyone has a position and there is a strategy to get them to the next place. We have to seek God to find out what the best move is for us. I was positioned in a certain city at a certain time to have a certain event to happen to me in order for me to seek God.

Beloved, I wish above all things that thou mayest prosper and be in health, even as thy soul prospereth, (3 John 2 KJV).

If God says that He wishes above ALL things that we prosper, then it is His intention that we prosper! I believe He wants us to be successful financially, physically, spiritually, and mentally.

Fearfully and wonderfully made

I praise you because I am fearfully and wonderfully made; your works are wonderful, I know that full well, (Psalm 139:14 NIV).

I love this Bible verse. It lets me know that when God made me He didn't make a mistake. He created me just the way He wanted me to be. For a long time I struggled with the way I looked. I didn't like the shape of my nose, I thought my eyes were too small and my skin was too dark. I let the way people treated me dictate how I felt about myself. When someone would say "You would be cute if you weren't so dark" or "You're cute to be so dark," I took it to heart. My self- esteem was so low.

I walked with my head down and I was very timid. I'm so glad I finally know who I am and whose I am.

For God has not given you a spirit of fear; but of power, and of love, and of a sound mind" (2 Timothy 1:7 AKJV)

I am naturally quiet, but no longer timid. I use my voice to glorify God wherever I go.

For we are His workmanship, created in Christ unto good works, which God hath ordained that we should walk in them. Ephesians 2:10

I no longer struggle with the way that I look. I am God's workmanship. He gave me my father's eyes and skin complexion. My nose is a combination of his and my mother's and I'm ok with that. I will no longer insult God by being dissatisfied with His workmanship.

I pray that my story blesses and helps someone. If you are going through depression, there is help out there. Talk to someone like your pastor, a trusted friend, or family member and get help. I suffered in silence for so long and never reached out for help. I thank God that He had a plan for my life and I am still here to help someone, because He said, *"Live!"*

If you're contemplating suicide, there is a national suicide prevention line that you can call and talk to someone. Remember, God has plans to prosper you and to give you hope and a future!

National Suicide Prevention Lifeline 1-800-273-8255

Endnotes:
Jeremiah 29:11 (NIV)
3 John 2 (KJV)
2 Timothy 1:7 (AKJV)
Psalm 3:5 (NKJV)
Psalm 139:14 (NIV)
Ephesians 2:10 (KJV)

The Lord your God will bring you into the land which your fathers possessed, and you shall possess it; and He will prosper you and multiply you more than your fathers.

Deuteronomy 30:5

Kristy L. Jones

First time author **Kristy L. Jones**, is passionate about education and helping people overcome adversity in order to reach their goals. She is a native of Marion, Indiana, and a proud graduate of Indiana Wesleyan University, where she received both her Bachelor and Master degrees. Kristy gained her teaching experience at Lawrence North and North Central High Schools both in Indianapolis, Indiana.

In 2013, she became an administrator at Andrew J. Brown Academy, where she contributed to the school's turnaround efforts, moving the school's state letter grade from an F to a C. Currently, she is an Assistant Principal at George Buck Elementary School.

Kristy's passion, combined with her experiences as an educator and young, single parent, led her to the establishment of *Spirit of the Village, Inc.*, a 501(c)3 not-for-profit organization committed to strengthening and supporting the family unit through community partnership and involvement, parent empowerment, educational development, and youth engagement. The organization's vision is to "restore the spirit of the village," which she believes will have a positive impact on the community as a whole.

Kristy is a daughter, sister, mother, auntie, and friend, and ultimately, she is an ambassador for Christ. She is on a journey to share His message by sharing her story, demonstrating His love, and by walking in His will and purpose for her life.

CHAPTER FOUR

Called to Love

It was August 23, 2014, I had just done my last glance over Brittany's dorm to make sure she had everything she needed before I left her to begin her journey as a student at Tennessee State University, the Land of the Golden Sunshine. We said our goodbyes, hugged, and I walked myself out. I was determined not to cry as everyone said I would. I sat in my car for a few minutes before pulling off, thinking about how faithful God had been to me.

You see, at the ripe young age of 15, two days before my sweet 16th birthday, I gave birth to my sweet baby girl, Brittany Janae. For the past 18 years, I spent my life trying to redeem myself by creating a life that everyone would be proud of since I had "messed up" by having a child as a teenager and out of wedlock.

I had also spent the past 18 years trying to break the cycle of teenage pregnancy in my family by doing everything in my power to prevent Brittany from becoming a teenage mother. And here I was, moving my daughter into her first choice for college, which also happened to be my first choice. It began to rain, but the sun did not stop shining. As I watched the rain drops and sun rays hit my window, a sense of accomplishment overwhelmed me and all I could do was thank God!

I thanked Him for helping me finish high school with honors, receiving nine scholarships, receiving my bachelor's degree, master's degree, and principal licensure certificate through Indiana Wesleyan University, building my house at the age of 26, raising a god-fearing, intelligent, and divinely talented daughter who does not have any children and is going to college. I did it!

My New Normal

The beginning of my drive home was pleasant, but the closer I got to home the more I did not want to be there. For the last hour of the drive, I cried uncontrollably; I thought I was going to have to pull over to get myself together. I did not go home; instead, I went to the arms of a man I was dating at the time. I knew he did not love me, but his embrace gave me a false sense of love, and in that moment, I was okay with that. In fact, I had been okay with it for over a year and planned to continue to be in order to avoid being "alone."

I began planning for my empty nest during Brittany's senior year; the more independent she became, the more worthless I felt. I stepped down from being the leader of the young adult ministry at church because my job was so demanding, which worked out for me...at least I thought.

When Brittany went to college, I started skipping church some Sundays to avoid answering people's insensitive questions and small talk about how I was doing without Brittany. Also, Sundays were my not so busy days, so I had more time to think about Brittany. I would lay in the bed and cry, thinking about not only her, but my Grandma Jones as well. She went home to be with the Lord about three weeks before I took Brittany to college. I had never imagined life without her; in my mind, she was immortal and would always be there. I felt guilty for not spending as much time with her in my adult life as I probably should have.

By December, I added the stress of work and the absence of friends including the man I was dating to my list of things to be sad about on Sunday mornings. My plan of consuming my day with work during the day, dinner with friends in evening, and lustful nights with "my" man was not working! Instead, work was chaotic and draining, my friends were busy with their own lives and "my" man had lost interest. Now what? I spent the remainder of the school year in what I recognize now as depression, with temporary relief over the summer when Brittany was home. But, come fall, I was back to my new normal. I put on a happy face during the day and was depressed through the night and on Sundays.

God Is Faithful

The climax of my depression was proceeded by a time that I like to call #Godisfaithful! During this time, God dropped moments into my memory of when He proved He was faithful, like the time He kept me from becoming a statistic as the product of divorced parents. Or, the time He saved my mom's life and protected my sisters and I from witnessing the abuse she received from her husband.

God was faithful when He allowed our parents to

recover from the messy custody battle which resulted in my mom's favor, (which was our preference as well), not overlooking the fact that I had a father who cared enough to fight for me in the first place.

Furthermore, He demonstrated His faithfulness when He followed through with His promise to help me raise Brittany, keeping her from becoming a statistic as the product of unwed, teenage parents and avoided becoming one herself. Most recently, His faithfulness was proven when He made a way out of no way by providing a means for me to finance her college experience; allowing me to be a Tennessee State Mom since I chose not to be a Tennessee State student. This "faith file" check opened my eyes and caused me to start looking at the natural supernaturally. I believe it was God's way of reminding me that He brought me through before, and He would do it again!

I spent my life trying to redeem myself by creating a life that everyone would be proud of since I had "messed up" by having a child as a teenager and out of wedlock.

In addition, God connected me to three women with whom I developed very distinct, meaningful relationships. I met each of the women at different times at my job. Later, I connected all three women, and we began to call ourselves "Girlfriends in God," GIG for short. I will not go into detail about each woman's story, but God used their stories to teach me how to love, rather than judge. He allowed me to witness first hand His power to transform the lives of those who choose to seek

Him. Moreover, He showed me the importance of putting ourselves in a position to hear from Him and respond by being obedient as He used me as a vessel in their lives as well.

The time I spent with two of my GIG's daughters helped me cope with missing my own. My GIG's were my support system throughout my transformation and as I dealt with a stressful working environment. Many times I wanted to quit, but I knew I was on assignment.

My level of stress reached an all-time high right around the time Alex and Stephen Kendrick's movie, "War Room" was released. I was inspired by the character portrayed by Priscilla Shirer, and I made a decision to abide in God's will and purpose for my life even if it meant I had to "suffer"; it was only when God said *move* that I would move. I committed to spending each morning in the Word and prayer, something I had never been able to do consistently, but I knew it was necessary if I wanted to hear from God.

The more I read the Word, the stronger I felt. God put it on my heart to reach out to one of a handful of people I refer to as my BFF, (best friend forever). I distanced myself from her because I was extremely vulnerable and emotional, and I was not capable of presenting myself as the strong woman she knew. When she did not reach out as often as I thought she should, I felt like she abandoned me at a time when I needed her most. However, God helped me see that there were some people He needed to disconnect me from because I was depending too much on them to help me cope with my empty nest syndrome. He wanted me to depend solely on Him.

On several occasions, we caught up on the phone and over dinner. As she filled me in on what had been going on in her life, I realized that this was a real-life illustration of something my BFF would say often, "Perception is reality." In this moment, God taught me that in every situation, I need to consider all perspectives before making a judgement. She had her own story to tell, and I could understand how she could have felt as if I abandoned her. I allowed the enemy to turn a situation that God clearly had His hand on into an "it's all about me" situation; He taught me long ago that it is not!

I had never experienced a love like this, and not only did I want more, I wanted others to experience this love as well.

God is Love

While scrolling through Facebook one day, I came across a video of Jada Pinkett-Smith being interviewed by her daughter Willow. Willow asked, "How hard is it being a wife and a mother?" One thing stuck out to me in her response. She explained how she had forgotten how to take care of herself when her children were born because they were her world. At that moment, I realized I had never learned how to take care of myself. I had gone from being taken care of by my parents to taking care of Brittany, which was why having an empty nest was difficult for me.

This revelation made it clear to me how I got to where I was at the beginning of this journey. Knowing how I got there helped me understand what work I needed to do to move forward. I used the following scriptural references to help guide me through this work:

- *Search me, O God, and know my heart; test me and know my anxious thoughts. Point out anything in me that offends you, and lead me along the path of everlasting life* (Psalms 139:23-24).
- *Don't copy the behavior and customs of this world, but let God transform you into a new person by changing the way you think. Then you will learn and know God's will for you, which is good and pleasing and perfect* (Romans 12:2 ESV).
- *...I focus on this one thing: Forgetting the past and looking forward to what lies ahead, I press on to reach the end of the race and receive the heavenly prize for which God, through Christ Jesus, is calling us* (Philippians 3:13b,14 ESV).

Throughout this journey, I learned a lot about myself and God. As I studied affirmations in the Bible, I began to gain a better understanding of who I was and how God saw me. I began to become more comfortable and content with my appearance and personality. I began to recognize my value, allowing my relationships with friends, co-workers, and family to change. I stopped wanting to please people and was intentional about making sure my decisions and actions pleased God. I realized I did not have to redeem myself from becoming an unwed, teenage parent because God already did that for me, as the song says, "way back on Calvary"; nor, do I have to settle for false love, because God's love for me is real.

Each time I studied the Word, offered up praise,

and/or spent time in worship, the more I felt Him loving on me, and I loved Him back. I had never experienced a love like this, and not only did I want more, I wanted others to experience this love as well.

I became more intentional about my interactions with people, being careful not to be judgmental, speaking only when God prompted me to speak, learning to understand people by viewing things from their perspective, and allowing God to use me to bless others. I went back to consistently attending church, tithing, and participating in ministry. I committed to submitting to His will and trusting Him in all areas of my life. As a result, God gave me a new identity along with a new name. Love, to remind me of His love for me, to remember to operate in love with others, and as a reminder to love myself. No longer do I feel worthless; it is my calling to love!

Prayer

My prayer is the same prayer Paul prayed in Ephesians 3:16-19 (ESV),

I pray that from his glorious, unlimited resources he will empower you with inner strength through his Spirit. Then Christ will make his home in your hearts as you trust in him. Your roots will grow down into God's love and keep you strong. And may you have the power to understand, as all God's people should, how wide, how long, how high, and how deep his love is. May you experience the love of Christ, though it is too great to understand fully. Then you will be made complete with all the fullness of life and power that comes from God.

Endnotes:
Psalms 139:23-24
Romans 12:2
Philippians 3:13b,14
Ephesians 3:16-19

Cassemdreia "Missy" O'Neal

Cassemdreia "Missy" O'Neal is first a child of God.

She is also a loving wife to Jerry and mother to three beautiful children: Jaiah, Cassidy, and Jaiden. She is a proud granddaughter, daughter, goddaughter, niece, sister, cousin, auntie, friend, and mentor. She was raised by her single mother Karen Clayborn as her father T. Smith fought a battle of his own.

After years of sexual abuse, she later left her mother's home and spent time in foster care/group home, later adopted by her Auntie Arnetra and Uncle Randolph Rhodes. In 2003, she graduated from Broad Ripple High School. She attended Indiana State College and later finished at MedTech College.

She's a member of Life Church of Brownsburg. She loves being a positive model to her children who look up to her as their mother. She enjoys crafts, traveling, gardening, hanging with her family and catching up with her cousins and friends. She loves spending time with her nieces and nephews.

Melissa.
Thank You.
Missy

CHAPTER FIVE

Journey

Out of Sight But in My Mind

Curling up in a ball, clutching the covers to somehow hide herself, she began to cry. "No, please not again. Please stop! Get off me! You're hurting me!"

He covered her mouth. She gasped for air. He continued to hold the pillow over her face. Her faint cries for help going unheard in the night. She struggled to breathe as she kept hitting, kicking, and pushing his broad shoulders off her petite frame. She could feel herself becoming weaker the harder she fought. Then, her body went limp.

Suddenly I was awakened by a familiar faint voice and a cold towel on my forehead. I began to flood my pillow with tears. Crying and apologizing to my husband, he quickly hugged me and in his sweet gentle tone reassured me I was safe and was having a nightmare.

This was more than a nightmare. It was my past coming back to torment me. As the days became shorter, the nights became longer and I grew more scared and felt unsafe. I was easily frightened and always on guard.

I started to push people away. The further I pushed people away the closer "he," the man from my nightmare, came. I was alone in a room full of people because I trusted no one. Everyone and anyone could hurt me or my children. I was extremely over-protective of them. I would mentally survey my surroundings, always on the defensive, just in case.

Believe

Some nights I would not go to sleep. The fear of what sleep would bring paralyzed me. My rushing thoughts wouldn't allow me to rest. I would constantly check the doors throughout the night as everyone else slept. Many nights my husband would wake up and ask, "How long have you been awake?" I would never tell him the truth. I didn't want him to worry about me.

One morning over breakfast, my husband asked me the unthinkable. "What are your nightmares about?" Sipping my coffee, I did not know how to answer him. I was nervous at the thought of revealing my innermost darkest secret, a secret I had held on to for 22 years out of fear of rejection.

I slowly opened my mouth. The words would not come out. My husband tried to read my lips as I drifted away in my thoughts. Before he knew it, I was drenched in sweat and gasping for air. The sound of his deep soft voice brought me back to reality.

My nightmares had now invaded my day. As I looked around, I realized I was at home. Confused, ashamed, and embarrassed, my eyes met his. I was waiting for him to say something. He just grabbed my hand and led me to the bookshelf. He reached for the Bible. As he opened it he looked at me and said, "Let's pray, repeat after me."

Heal me, O LORD, and I will be healed; save me and I will be saved, for you are the one I praise. Jeremiah 17:14

As I repeated after him I felt a huge weight lifted off my shoulders. He encouraged me to read the Bible more often. He reminded me that he would wait patiently until I was ready to share my nightmares.

I felt safety and comfort within the walls of the church. Life felt better, the sun shined brighter, the birds even chirped louder.

In the following days, I read my Bible before bed. Flipping through the pages, I would randomly stop at different verses. Praying God would send me to the verse I needed to read.

"For his anger endureth but a moment; in his favour is life: weeping may endure for night, but joy cometh in the morning." Psalm 30:5 King James Version.

After reading, I placed my Bible on the nightstand and laid in bed. Thinking how the verse related to my life. For the first time in months I drifted off to a peaceful sleep. Waking up rested, I expected immediate change. I went on about my days with a new determination to be free.

No Weapons Formed Against Me Shall Prosper

Sunday morning started with breakfast before the family headed out in search of a church home, kind of like the one I grew up in. After two months of searching, we attended an event and received a friendly invitation to visit New Life Church. The church greeted us in a unique, personable way. We continued to visit the church more often. Engaging in activities inside and outside the church, I began to feel safe and started letting my guard down.

One evening while in the grocery store, I was checking out and a familiar smell of musky cologne triggered a memory. All of a sudden, I was back in my nightmare gasping for air, heart racing, and sweaty palms. I was hallucinating, trying to think of a way out! Someone taps my shoulder. Instantly I run from the store. I'm fumbling with my keys trying to get into my car, only to realize it's not my car. I run across the parking lot, jump in the car and begin crying out to God, "HELP ME! HELP ME! HELP ME! It's happening again."

Calm comes over me and I realize no one is after me; it's a panic attack.

Though frightening, I couldn't allow a panic attack to stop the progress I had made. I continued attending church and we made New Life our church home. I felt safety and comfort within the walls of the church. Life felt better, the sun shined brighter, the birds even chirped louder.

Deep within my heart I struggled with forgiveness, guilt, and shame because of what I encountered in my past. I desperately sought healing. For the first time in my adult life, I felt no shame asking for prayer and guidance. I sought counsel from Pastor Denis Roy, hoping he could lead me in the right direction. I shared some of my childhood issues and my struggles with forgiveness, guilt, and shame. He prayed against spiritual warfare, he also prayed all soul ties and chains be broken.

Faith

That evening I began to share my 22-year secret, the source of my nightmares, with my husband. I told him of the sexual abuse. I told him how my nights were filled with fear and could I not sleep. Even now, my subconscious remembered the abuse like it was still happening. When sleep came, I would wake up fighting for my life just like I was nine years old again. This is what I was carrying. This is what tormented my nights and was now threatening my days. For the first time, I was able to speak the words to someone without fear of rejection. Tears of joy filled my eyes as I continued to share with my husband. Finally, the demon that haunted me was exposed. I was released from the prison of my past. I was free from shame.

For months to come, I found comfort in knowing I was back. Back from living in shame and in guilt, with the openness of my heart to forgive. My church family prayed for our family and it felt good knowing I wasn't alone. The more I attended church the more my soul was fed. As time passed my spirit grew stronger. Before I knew it, I was sharing how God has and is still blessing me. My life isn't the same. If it wasn't for God and his faithfulness to me, I would still be in the dark place of my past. God never changed, even when I changed. He is the same God I met years ago.

"Jesus Christ is the same yesterday and today and forever." Hebrew 13:8.

Sharing My Testimony of Patience

My innocence was taken away from me at the age of nine. I suffered years of sexual abuse while in my mother's home. My abuser was always around. He was an accepted part of my family. As a child, I tried to tell people, but no one listened. There was no safe place for me go. I finally was placed in a foster care/group home setting and later adopted by Arnetra and Randolph Rhodes, my aunt and uncle. This was my escape.

My abuser was out of sight, but never out of mind. He became my deep, dark secret that haunted me well into my adult years. I began fighting off my abuser in my nightmares only to wake up in a panic-stricken state. Every time I'd flashback it was like I was watching myself be molested. I could feel the pain and panic all over again. It was a part of my existence. I lived the shame and guilt of it every day. Something as minor as my husband moving in bed easily triggered me in my sleep. During the day, a smell or thought would take me back.

Watching my daughter turn nine years old was terrifying. Terrifying, because she reminded me of my-self when I was her age and I wanted to be healed NOW! As I sought healing Gods timing was important.

"He said to them: It is not for you to know the times or dates the Father has set by his own authority." Acts 1:7

I needed patience and an open mind. I felt love and support as my church family wrapped their arms around me. Comfort allowed me to progress to see a therapist. Embracing my childhood issues allowed me to forgive myself first. I took small steps, ultimately forgiving my abuser.

I went through many of years of counseling for depression and anxiety; Post-Traumatic Stress Disorder (PTSD) was new for me. I had many years of experience working at Damar Residential Services with teenage girls living with behavioral and developmental disabilities. I often encouraged these young ladies to push through PTSD symptoms.

God was already setting my steps for my journey. I didn't understand how my childhood problems suddenly appeared in my adult life. I met weekly with a trauma therapist at Cummins Behavior Health Center.

As trust was built between Tom, my therapist, and I, I was able to open up a little more each time. He helped me to understand trauma and its effects. It was tough remembering the abuse and the abuser, yet I became more confident as I slowly worked through my fears, the nightmares, and panic attacks.

Finally, the demon that haunted me was exposed. I was released from the prison of my past. I was free from shame.

Today I'm very grateful God sent me a patient husband; one that loved me even when I didn't know how to love myself. He was there when I pushed my family and friends away. I trusted no one around my children. I lived in fear that someone was going to hurt them. I was on guard countless nights. Alone with guilt and shame, I began to seek God. I started my mornings reading the *Daily Bread* devotional and ended with the Bible. I started seeing improvements in my days and nights. I was better, but I still needed more healing.

It took a village of God's children from different walks of life to help me heal. In return, I have met some amazing people along the way. I am thankful for my journey with all the ups, the downs, and the in-between.

I'm certainly not where I want to be, yet I'm grateful for not being where I used to be. I'm still a work in progress. God's love has made me better, not bitter. I'm still learning to love myself and trust others around my children. I'm learning the difference between being aware and being guarded.

Today, the burden of my past is lifted. The little girl in me that suffered so much is now healed. We both are at peace. I sleep at night. I can watch my children play without excessive concern. Embracing my authentic identity, I am finally free to be me, the dynamic woman I was created to be. I am now, Positioned to Prosper!

God, my God, I yelled for help and you put me together. God, you pulled me out of the grave, gave me another chance at life when I was down-and-out. Psalm 30:2-3 MSG

No More Fear

Lastly, I want to speak to anyone who has or is experiencing abuse of any kind. You are not designed to live in fear. Know that you do have a choice. You have a say in how your life will turn out. This is not your identity; this will not define you. You can overcome every obstacle in your past and be healed. Don't be afraid to ask for help. Find someone you can trust and confide in. Refuse to be tormented any longer. Expose the enemy of your soul. It is the only way to start your journey to healing. The road will have many twists and turns, but with the help of God and your support system, you too will be made whole.

Prayer:

Blessed is the man that walketh not in the counsel of the ungodly, nor standeth in the way of sinners, nor sitteth in the seat of the scornful. 2 *But his delight is in the law of the Lord; and in his law doth he meditate day and night.* 3 *And he shall be like a tree planted by the rivers of water, that bringeth forth his fruit in his season; his leaf also shall not wither; and whatsoever he doeth shall prosper.* 4 *The ungodly are not so: but are like the chaff which the wind driveth away.* 5 *Therefore the ungodly shall not stand in the judgment, nor sinners in the congregation of the righteous.* 6 *For the Lord knoweth the way of the righteous: but the way of the ungodly shall perish.*
Psalm 1-6 KJV

Choyce Shania Guice-Robertson

Choyce Shania Guice-Robertson has found that her purpose is to serve and help others to "position to prosper!"

Choyce, a sincerely caring young woman, made her entrance into the world on April 1, 1990. She is the daughter of Shatira Guice and Timothy D. Hanson; the eldest sister of five other siblings; the wife of Minister Jarvay H. Robertson; the mother of Tyree, Mitzie, and the newest addition to the family, Jace Jamal Robertson. Her children and family are her driving force and source of encouragement.

Even as a young child, Choyce was passionate about caring for people. After graduating from Firestone High School, she enrolled in North Coast Medical Training Academy and became a LPN. She started her career loving and caring for the elderly, all the while knowing God was calling her deeper.

She is positioning herself for the "deeper." Choyce is studying human behavior at IVY Tech to become a counselor. To further push herself into destiny, Choyce received her certification as a coach and consultant with Authentic Institute. She is actively using her training to help transform the lives of others to become the best that they can be. She is working to start MIA (Minorities in Autism), a support group for families of individuals that have ASD (Autism Spectrum Disorder).

CHAPTER SIX

Knowledge is Power

Recently I was presented with a thought provoking question. The question was so simple, yet pierced through my soul. The answer was clear right away. Almost immediately my eyes and ears were opened. I could hear God precisely and see His vision for my life so clearly.

The question? What three things do you value most in life?

My answer? 1. My relationship with God; 2. My children; 3. My education

The answer was clear, but the journey to get to that answer was not an easy one. It wasn't until I began explaining the reason behind my choices and their order did I realize everything I've gone through, the struggles I faced, and the period of not knowing who I was, all had purpose. A specific design to bring me to God's expected end. Him, behind the scenes positioning me to prosper.

My foundation in religion began early. My grandmother instilled in me Christian values and a spirit of excellence. She never allowed me to give anything less than my best. I did not know at the time how those three things would carry me through life. My grandmother had grown up Jehovah's Witness. She taught me the basics of prayer, who my creator is, and the purpose of Jesus dying on the cross. I went to Catholic school and attended religion classes. On Sundays, my grandmother made sure I was up and on the church bus to attend Sunday school at the Baptist church around the corner. My foundation was being formed through three different views of who God is. I was aware of God, but I did not know God. This is key…

I did not come from a traditional family. I was raised by my grandmother. My mother was fairly young when she had me. She left me in the care of my grandmother to finish her education at Job Corp. When she returned she was with child again and had not completed her education at the time. I remained in my grandmother's custody. This situation caused my heart to be divided. My grandmother was my mother but I couldn't call her mom. I loved my mother like a mom, but I couldn't live with her. I only visited my mom when she and my grandmother could agree to disagree. I know they both loved me and only wanted the best for me, but I spent most of my childhood torn between the two.

Growing up the oldest of six children, I took pride in being a big sister. In fact, to this day, I place high value on being a big sister, mother, nurse, wife, aunt, daughter, and granddaughter. I proudly wear each title and take the responsibility of each seriously. So much so, I neglect me. I have this image of myself dancing around in my head that tells me I'll be seen as weak if I can't handle the pressure. My entire identity is tied up in these titles. Without them who would I be? My family defined me.

I never knew the love of a father. The first time I met my father, I was seven years old. He just showed up one day as I was visiting one of my mother's friends. I remember it so well; I was called to the front porch. A man was walking towards the house. The lady on the porch said, "That's your daddy." Without hesitation, I jumped off the porch and ran to him yelling DADDY! I clung to him for dear life. He took me for a ride and we talked. At seven there wasn't much to say but it didn't matter. The moment I had secretly dreamed about was finally here. I had a father!

Five or six years later he announces that he, my sister and brother were moving to California. What? Leaving? Without me? Why? My mind was on tilt. I couldn't understand how he could just up and leave me. We were just getting to know one another. He promised me I could visit during school breaks and summer vacations. NO! That was not acceptable, but what could I do? I was only a child who wanted to be with her father.

The visits never happened.

Four years went by and I was given the opportunity to move to California. Once again, my heart leaped for joy. I was getting my father back. After being there for two months I was hospitalized, where we discovered I was pregnant. I was 16, in pain, lying in a hospital bed away from home. My father didn't take the news of my pregnancy well. He accused us of tricking him by sending me to live with him, knowing I was pregnant. That was not the case. There was no reasoning with him. I decided to go back home to Ohio. I had an abortion and never saw or talked to my father again. I have attempted to reach out to him over the last 12 years but he has totally disowned me.

Being abandoned by my father and my distant relationship with my mother left a void in me that I didn't understand. I felt disconnected. My heart was in a desolate place. I wasn't really sure who I was. I was hungry for relationship. I yearned to be accepted. I wanted to be needed. I wanted love!

One day, at the age of 19, the right words were whispered in my ear, my heart melted. I knew this boy would never leave me. I had finally found love. In 2009, I gave birth to my first child, a son. My world was now perfect. I had a man who was always there for me when family dynamics were at their worst and took care of all my physical and emotional needs. This had to be love!

Take heed, my friends. If you are in a situation even remotely similar to this, leave before you get in too deep.

It wasn't until a year after my son's birth that my eyes were opened to the reality of this relationship. I was lying in a hospital bed with black and blue eyes, bruises all over my body, and a broken nose, in a state of confusion. How could this man who loved me and I loved, do this to me? My mind was so bound…my soul was tied to this man. All I wanted to do was to talk to him and fix this mess. I wanted to go back.

God's plan is to bring me to an expected end. His expected end, and this was not it. God's plan for me did not involve this man or his abuse, but would serve a purpose in my journey. Because I didn't really know God, I could not recognize all the warning signs. God was right there saying, right in the face of the enemy, "It's not over!" In Job 1:8 God asks Satan, "Have you considered my servant Job?" It's so thought provoking to think that Satan actually has to ask permission before he can try God's people. By the grace of God, I walked away from this relationship a little wiser and with a better understanding of who God is…My Healer.

My heart was still tender. My soul still fragmented, yet my relationship with God growing stronger. It was in this vulnerable state God allowed me to be tested. I met a man, twenty years older. Mature, caring, kindhearted, and charismatic with a genuine interest in my well-being.

This man was my provider. I was in school and had no worries. He paid all my bills, made sure I had all I needed. He was my protector. No one could harm me. I felt safe with him. He was everything to me. Little did I realize he was my greatest danger. He said to me one day, "You praying to God is fine but I make shit happen." He thought he was God. A very clear sign to run for my life, but I was in too deep. I wouldn't hear from him for weeks, even months, but I kept going back. I couldn't leave him. I decided to move in with him.

There's a special lady I highly respect and value her opinion. She called me one day. Her tone was serious; questioning my decision to move in with this man. She quoted scriptures and talked about this decision. I listened to what she had to say. I told her "This is going to be my husband. He wants to marry me. I am finally going to have my own family."

Take heed, my friends. If you are in a situation even remotely similar to this, leave before you get in too deep. Listen to your friends and family. God is speaking to you through them. Like me, you can't see what is really going on. You're in too deep and your judgement is altered. I couldn't hear God speaking through someone I greatly admired and would have normally listened to.

Five years of pure hell! I was being controlled by this man, spirit, soul, and body. There we so many mind games. Sometimes I didn't even know who I was or where I was going. I was in a daze. A dark cloud surrounded me. My life was filled with sleepless nights, dark shadows and many, many tears. Men defined me. But God!

God's mercy came and found me right there in that dark place. He allowed me to see literally every man in my life had hurt me, failed me, and left me beat down and broken. He delivered me. That empty place I was talking about earlier is now filled to the full with God's Holy Spirit. I now have a relationship with Him. I know who He is and I know who I am with Him. He is my Father! He is my Provider, not a man! He is my Protector, not a man! He defines me, not another person! He is the only one who will never leave me nor forsake me. My heart is chained and only God has the key.

Through all this drama, I bet you're wondering, where are her children in all of this? I never gave up on being a mother. My children were and are my inspiration. I get up and try again everyday so my children may have a better life with a brighter future.

I have three children, one with special needs. Being a parent is no easy task. Being a single parent makes it even more challenging. But having a special needs child takes parenting to another level.

My child was diagnosed with ADHD and put on several medications. Well-meaning individuals offered advice on how to "handle" my child. Some suggested he would grow out of it. Some suggested I just "whip his butt." The doctors and teachers, just medicate him. None of these solutions were viable. There was more going on with my son. The battle began!

I educated myself about programs, treatments, medications, and health insurance. I sought out the best treatment and doctors for my son. I've had to fight my way through the special education system for many school terms. We've been kicked out of programs and flat out rejected by some because they were not equipped to handle my child's needs. I have had to quit jobs to sit in countless meetings and monitor classrooms.

Sometimes I didn't have the support of family and friends, but I couldn't let that stop me. Finally, my prayers were answered. The correct diagnosis of Autism was given and a suitable treatment plan established. The journey was fierce and sometimes lonely, but the end result is worth every battle and every struggle.

Because God equipped me with a tenacious spirit, my child is doing well today. It's now two years without any medications other than vitamins.

If you are the parent/parents of a unique child, don't settle for the status quo. Advocate for your child! Educate yourself! Get a FULL understanding. Don't stop at one opinion. Keep going until you get the result that is right for your child.

With all the challenges I faced, being a mom is never a burden. I will tell you, everything you go through affects your children in some way, whether you realize it or not. Some scars cannot be seen by the natural eye, but are felt deeply in their spirits. I can only trust

God to heal every wounded place within my children caused by my mistakes.

With that being said, I see the importance of a two-parent household. I understand now that a single parent household does not mean it has to be dysfunctional. I came from a dysfunctional family, but my children do not have to live with dysfunction. It is my responsibility to assure the same things that held me in bondage do not bind my children. I thank God he has placed a caring man in my life to be a husband to me and father to my children.

Every single parent reading this; get close to your children. Listen to their tears. Understand their fears. Pray for them. Break every bondage and generational curse operating against them. Ask God daily to destroy chains, break relationships up, and remove anything attached to your lineage that has the potential to detour your children from their destiny in Him.

For me, that meant removing all the men in my life, including my father, so that I could know Him as Father, Protector, Provider, and the true Lover of my soul. God is a jealous God and will not allow another to steal His glory. Now my children will know Him. My daughter will never have to experience the heartbreak from a man that I did. She will understand the love and affection she seeks can only come from God. The only love that is unconditional and everlasting. Sure, she will have choices and will make mistakes. She will not fall through the cracks. Her foundation will be solid. This goes for my son as well. He will not fall prey to any woman. He will know what a virtuous woman looks like because he will see her in me.

Education begins in the womb and continues until death. Babies are learning from their mother. They learn the rhythm of her heart and the sound of her voice. When they are born, the connection is there.

I believe my desire to learn, seek answers, and look for solutions has kept me standing through adversity.

Life is a learning continuum. Every day you open your eyes is an opportunity to learn something new. Whether from a book, a teacher or online, the chance to educate yourself on a wide variety of subjects is available to you.

My grandmother taught me to value education. When learning was difficult, she hired a tutor. When projects were due, she stayed up late to help me with the finishing touches. She always told me "knowledge is power." I now understand that the power is not in education itself. The power is in the knowledge received from education. Knowledge is education at work. (perhaps 'in action')

I believe my desire to learn, seek answers, and look for solutions has kept me standing through adversity. The wisdom I received from God, even when I didn't know or understand, has kept me moving forward. I value my education and pray I never lose the desire to learn more.

It doesn't matter how old you are, how many children you have, how much money you have or your status in life, it's never too late to get an education. Nothing is impossible with God.

Now, 27 years old, I still have a lot to learn and a lot to give. My relationship with God is my first priority. Without it, I have no direction. I lose my identity and have no purpose. Through my relationship with God, I am a better parent. I am able to recognize spiritual roadblocks that can detour my children from the path of success and guide them. Through my relationship with God I am able to conquer educational barriers, paving the way for my children and others. I understand that education is important, but knowledge is power. Because I know Him, God uses my relationship with Him, my children and everything I learn, in and out of a classroom, to bring me to His expected end. I am "Positioned to Prosper" because of it.

And we know that in all things God works for the good of those who love him, who have been called according to his purpose.

Romans 8:28

Jarvay Hsan Rudy Robertson

Minister Jarvay Hsan Rudy Robertson believes that a major part of his destiny is to use his testimony to help change the lives of young people.

Jarvay is the son of Jamal V. Robertson and Jermaine L. O'Conner. Born in Milwaukee, Wisconsin, on October 5, 1989, he is happily married to Choyce Guice-Robertson.

Minister Robertson is a leader, preacher, teacher, and motivational speaker. He is the proud father of three beautiful children Tyree, Mitzie, and newest addition, Jace Jamal Robertson.

Falling in love with God at the young age of three years old, his mother and family knew that his life would never be the same. He was baptized at the age of seven, fell in love with praise and worship, and directed his first choir at the age of eight., He began his training as a minister of the gospel under the leadership of Bishop Calvin B. Davis.

In 2008, Jarvay graduated from Muskegon Heights High School and then headed to Alabama State University to major in music education and biblical studies. That was also the year he gave God his Yes and was ordained. Jarvay credits his mother, and his wife's undying support as key to his work.

CHAPTER SEVEN

Finding Me

The Journey to Your Destiny

This chapter was written in a time in my life where I didn't know what I wanted, or where I wanted to be, and even worse, I couldn't determine who Jarvay Robertson was. I wanted to be great, but what does that look like for me? All my friends seemed happy, and it looked like they found their purpose in life. And even though I would smile and laugh, I always had a huge, larger-than-life-sized question mark in my soul; who are you? I needed to go on an inward journey to see.

Why did God put me here? Lauo Tzu said, "A journey of a thousand miles begins with one step." I felt like I was going to need a sports car just to start. We all have a place in life where we have to stop living from day to day and ask God, OK now what's my real purpose? I found that it's so hard to travel through life when you have no destination. You're just driving and eventually you run out of gas. I was stuck on the side of the road on empty. It's so bittersweet to say that this is the place where you actually start the journey to "finding Me."

The Breakdown

It's Thursday, 9:34 a.m., and it's raining outside. I'm late for work, broken down on the side of the road. I have my four-month old son in the car. The night before my wife told me, based upon my actions the last few months, that I may be suffering with depression. And I just had to ask simply, *Why today?* I found myself in a place of anger and frustration. I got even angrier that there were people reaching their destination, but for some reason I'm stuck, in the same place, and have been here for a while now. I called roadside assistance and for the first time they could not find my location because I was in such a weird place, now doesn't that speak to my life and how I'm feeling?

God now allows me to see my issues. Number one: for just a few minutes I was so focused on why other people were allowed to get to their destination without pause and I was stuck. God allowed me to see that to get where you are going you cannot worry about the ways other people are traveling. We see our friends, spouses, and those without faith, reaching some type of happiness or what we perceive to be happiness, that we tend to lose focus on our destiny and the road that we must travel. It is in this moment where I have to choose where I will put my focus. If I continue to focus on others I have just chosen to continue to stay stuck on the side of the road. Meanwhile, everyone else is driving.

Number two: I had no help! God put me in a position that I had to call on Him, in the moment when I fully realized that His wisdom was the only way out of this. The Bible says "... But seek ye first the kingdom of God, and his righteousness; and all these things shall be added unto you." In this life, we rely so much on other people, our phones. We want roadside assistance for our life. Every breakdown in life we call on everybody we know except the one who is really going to help us, and not judge us while He's doing it. Now while I'm stuck, the woman on the phone is no help, so I simply asked, "Can I call you back?"

She responds "sure."

I just start praying, "Lord what do I do?" Just as clear as day He says, "Move." This is the place where we come up with all of our excuses. I respond by saying, *I can't, cars are flying, it's raining, my tire is flat and coming off the rim, I can't move!*

He says again," Move."

I have come to believe that God puts us in the most awkward positions just to show us that he is God. He was trying to put me in the "Position to Prosper."

I move just 50 feet, at this point I'm able to see where I am, I'm actually in a safer spot. I call the woman back and ask, "Have you found out anything?"

" Yes, for some reason we now can pick up exactly where you are."

There is so much mess in my life right now, I feel like I can't even see God. My marriage is falling apart, and I have nothing to show for where I am.

If we take the time to call God first, and seek him for all the right things, then we allow Him to do what he does best. The way God does things often sound crazy to us. It's not about how he tells you to do it, more so it's about you just being obedient enough to get it done. Even though I'm still stuck on the side of the road I was at a place of understanding and that is the first step to getting to your destiny!

How did I get here?

What did I do to deserve this? How did I get to this place? Why me Lord? I am asking these questions and have no answer, but someone told me that "Sometimes God's silence is an answer."

There is so much mess in my life right now, I feel like I can't even see God. My marriage is falling apart, and I have nothing to show for where I am. I had no one to show me how to be a husband. I had no one to show me how to be a father. I have nothing. *Lord, how did I get to the place of being lost? Lord, you said that this was a part of my destiny, these are the things that you promised in your word to me.* Being broken-down left me with a feeling of being broken. *God, I did all that I knew how to do. How did I get to this place?* I would wake up in the mornings with the desire to do nothing. Have you ever found yourself in this place? What makes it so frustrating is that, you sometimes don't know how you got here, or why you are there. In that moment things seemed to be getting worse.

We have all been the place where we must, question ourselves and our beliefs. I saw that I was the problem, I had done so much to try to be perfect for everyone else. I've tried to meet everyone else's expectations of me that I have completely taken a detour off my road to my destiny. In the mist of trying to be what people said I should be, I somehow got completely thrown off of what

God has called me to be. I have been distracted by life and forgot who and what I was living for. I wasn't living for Him anymore! I was living for my wife, I was living for the church, I was living for success, I was living to remove the heartbreak of my father not being around, I was living to please people, I was living to overcome the generational curses over my life. The whole time that was somehow masked as if I was living for Him. I'm not saying these things are wrong, but we cannot forget God in all of this. When God has called you, when you have a destination to get to, it's the enemy's job to put road blocks, pot holes speed bumps, and whatever else he can to distract you from getting where you are going. When you find yourself stuck and attacked by the enemy, that's your first sign that you cannot give up.

The enemy doesn't bother those who are not a threat to his kingdom! When we become distracted God uses those very distractions to get our attention and move them out the way. His plan is the reason we live. You have to make up in your mind that from this moment that you will do whatever it takes to get to where you have to be. God said this in the book of Ezekiel.

And when I passed by you and saw you struggling in your own blood, I said to you in your blood, 'Live!' Yes, I said to you in your blood, 'Live!' Ezekiel 16 (KJV)

I say to you, I found this out - that God sees you in your mess. He knows your hurt, he knows your pain, but you are not your sin nor are you your past. These are the very things that got me off track. God says to you today *LIVE!* Even in your messy situation. Get up and live for him; he will do the cleaning up, he will wipe away your past, he will clean up the mess that you are in. I say to you, just as he has spoken to me, that he sees you struggle, he sees you in your own mess, and yet he still says *live*. It's time for you to realize that breakdowns come and hurt comes, but God has called you to live in it and through it. As you go through the fire you come out as pure gold. The first step to recovery is getting back on the road to destiny is living for Him.

Running out of Gas

There are only so many warning signs that can be given before you end up empty. We often find ourselves so busy that we miss these very signs. I feel that the worst thing in the world is having to be somewhere, or wanting to go somewhere and running out of gas. In my life, I knew that God had somewhere for me to be, I knew that my destiny was on the other side of my trouble, but I didn't have the fuel to get there. I wanted to make God proud of me. I wanted to show God that I could put to work all the great things that He has instilled in me. I found that trying to do anything on your own is a mistake.

We try too hard to be the next greatest thing and have not achieved what God has for us in this moment.

We need God! It's not an option at all. We have to recognize that He is the almighty, all powerful, all knowing God. He is the only reason we are able to become who he has called us to be. Even though God has given us the tools to be successful, we need his power to activate those tools. When I speak about "running out of gas" I'm not just speaking metaphorically; it also come in a very literal tone. We can try so hard to make it and forget who is the way maker. Push and push to become great, yet forget who the greatest is.

Some of you reading this chapter are emotionally empty, physically empty, financially empty. I found myself there, just to be transparent. We use more energy to do it on our own than we realize. I confess in this very moment as I write, this is where I am. I want to get to my destiny but I have no more gas. I'm on empty! I had to ask myself *Lord how did I get here?* I have been doing what I thought was right, and going in the direction that I thought I should go in and the whole time missing God.

For I know the plans I have for you, declares the LORD, plans to prosper you and not to harm you, plans to give you hope and a future. Jeremiah 29:11

I had to realize that God has the directions and the fuel to get me to where I need to be, not people, not family. We try too hard to be the next greatest thing and have not achieved what God has for us in this moment.

As you read this I want you to know that God sees you and hears you. You must remember that your way has already been made. God has mapped out every step, you do not have to just drive around aimlessly wondering what's next, you have the power and enough gas left in you to cry out to the Father to fill you up. The grace and mercy of God is more than enough.

Remember the power in the name of Jesus. Just because in this moment you feel like there is nothing left, I've found that's the very moment that God has just that much more. Sometimes God must allow us to empty ourselves of self to be refilled with Him. Find that last little bit of strength and call on Him because He has proven that He will never leave you nor forsake you.

Back on the road

I can only tell you in so many words that the story of my life has been full of so much hurt and pain that I felt like even though God has forgiven me and filled me back up I still felt like I wasn't good enough to carry out what God wanted me to do. I know that I'm not the only one in this position. In order for us to get back on the road to our destiny, we have to leave the past in their rearview mirror and look forward. You and I have the power put in us by God to do more than just get by, we have the power to make it. We have the power to win, in spite of what people, friends, or family may say. My favorite scripture says it best:

But the God of all grace, who hath called us unto his eternal glory by Christ Jesus, after that ye have suffered a while, make you perfect, stablish, strengthen, settle you. 1 Peter 5:10 (KJV)

Your suffering, hurt, and pain is not in vain; what doesn't break you will make you. These things must take place in order to put you in the "Position to Prosper." These passages show us that God has fully intended for us to know the pain of suffering, so that we may know the joy of getting to the destiny of which he has called us to. Those of you reading this should know that God is getting ready to make every situation in your life perfect. When God is the GPS system that is guiding us to our destination, the way that he has made will be perfect.

I always felt like I was last and counted out, even in my own personal family, but God speaks to us and says that he is getting ready to establish you. You will be the head and not the tail, the lender and not the borrower. All that you and I have been through, even though we did not understand it, God was providing us with the strength that we need to build what He has called us to build and go where He has called us to go.

My favorite of all is he is going to settle you, he will become your peace. He will become that everything that you need. I'm not telling you what I think, I'm telling you what I know and what I am seeing him do right now in my very own life. The change and transition may still be a little uncomfortable, but I must speak life. I have found that when you repeat God's word to him it wakes him up and calls attention to your issues.

Find the power that the world tried to take from you. Call on God like I did and he will answer. Let go of those things that bring you no peace. Live for God like you never have before. Push like you never have before. All that you go through is designed in His perfect plan for your life. If you find yourself in an off-road situation, call on his name.

It took me a while to find out that my praise and worship to God in my time of trouble confuses the enemy. No matter where you are on your journey, remember that God still is in control. My eyes are now open, I can see the destiny on the horizon. I can feel it in my soul. I have arrived at my destiny. Now that I am here the real work begins. I can go on and my suffering and pain was not in vain, but to prepare me for my arrival, and God is doing the same for you!

Prayer

Lord my God, I only know you to be a helper and a way maker. I ask that you would do for the reader just as you have done for me. God, I pray that you would be a light, even though it seems that every place that we walk in may be dark. God, I ask that you would relight the fire and the fight inside of our hearts. Lord, give us the strength to look up to you and call on your name. Father, even when I feel like we can no longer drive, Lord take over, because we know that you are the only one that can get us to our destiny. Lord, I decree and declare that we are winners. There will be success in our right now and our future. I pray Father that we are now in the "Position to Prosper!"

Endnotes:
Jeremiah 29:11 (KJV)
Ezekiel 16 (KJV)
1 Peter 5:10 (KJV)
Matthew 6:33 (KJV)

But the humble will inherit the land
And will delight themselves in abundant prosperity.
Psalm 37:11

Tiauna Ross

Tiauna Ross is a Michigan-based professional, career coach, author, speaker, and trainer who has created a niche in accounting, technology, and project management. She has over 13 years of experience in finance, accounting, project/program management, business and systems analysis, communication and change management.

She is known for her innovative and resourceful approach to managing people, projects, and systems, and her reputation for helping others achieve career success. She has led multiple award-winning projects throughout her career and has written articles for both the *PM Times* and *BA Times*. Tiauna actively works with individuals and groups to improve personal effectiveness through career coaching, mentoring, seminars, training, and personal development.

Tiauna earned a Master of Science Degree in Accountancy and Bachelor of Business Administration Degree, majoring in Accountancy & Personal Financial Planning, both from Western Michigan University. She completed the Stanford Advanced Project Management program in 2013 and is a Stanford Certified Project Manager, a Certified Public Accountant, a Certified Business Analysis Professional, and a Project Management Professional. She is also a Certified Human Behavioral Consultant and Certified 5D Coach through the Authentic Identity Institute.

Tiauna is a member of the Project Management Institute, the International Institute of Business Analysis and the Michigan Association of CPAs where she is contributor on the Program Curriculum, Management Information and Business Show, and Membership task forces.

CHAPTER EIGHT

A Road in the Wilderness

Every now and then, someone asks me how I got to where I am in my life. Honestly, my answer can be found in Isaiah 46:19 NKJV: *"Behold, I will do a new thing, now it shall spring forth; shall you not know it? I will even make a road in the wilderness and rivers in the desert."*

God made a road for me in the wilderness, and rivers in the desert when I was young. I don't know exactly how my life would have been different, but I know I would not be where I am today if God had not made a way for me.

My Foundation

When I look back over my foundation in life, I realize that I could have easily been a statistic. My mother was an unmarried 21-year-old when she discovered she was pregnant with me. She had completed a short tenure in the army and had returned to Benton Harbor, Michigan to build a life for herself. At the time I was conceived, she was working part-time at a discount store, to which she walked up and down a hill going to and from work. My father was on the verge of losing his mind, and unknown to him and anyone else at the time, he would never recover a full sense of sanity.

He was back from military service and had returned a stranger version of himself. He had a brilliant mind, well-versed in physics and mathematical complexities, but had somehow lost his ability to tolerate reality. Some say he told stories of being sprayed with a mysterious mist in open fields during his military service. Others believe the pressure he was under in the military drove him past his breaking point, especially considering as a child, he had witnessed the traumatic death of his own mother. Whether these beliefs are true or not, one thing was undeniable; he would never be the same again.

Unfortunately, he turned to alcohol as a young man as a coping mechanism. As such, he would become a background figure in my life, only represented in the form of old pictures and stories from other family members. I would be almost ten-years-old before I would meet him face-to-face. I don't know too much about my parent's relationship with each other, only that they knew each other from high school and were close in those young and impressionable days.

My mother would have to be fully responsible for the day-to-day work of raising me. She carried her own weight, but also had help from family to look after my brother and me while she worked. My grandmother lived next door during the early parts of my life, only to be a short walk through an open alley for the remainder of my childhood. I was never far from aunts, uncles, cousins, and other family members. I suspect that this kept the family surviving, with each of them just as dependent on the others.

Life was interesting for me as a kid. On one hand, I was growing up in a single parent home but didn't realize it until I was five-years-old. My mother found a new boyfriend when I was a baby and he became the man I know as my dad. He didn't have any children at that time, except for me, who he claimed as his own daughter in those early years. I was one of the fortunate ones. In my formative years, I was loved by a father figure and did not have to face the rejection of being abandoned until much later. My earliest memories involved me being at home with him, playing games and having fun. I remember being a small child when our kitchen caught on fire. He was the first one on the scene and protected us from the flames, ultimately being burned on his arms and face trying to contain the troubling fire.

For many years, we lived as a family and as far as I knew, things were just fine. I didn't notice signs of trouble until I overheard the makings of arguments coming from the other bedroom. These arguments began to increase in frequency and intensity. My dad struggled to find decent work and had periodic bouts of unemployment. He was home a lot of days with me. During other times, he worked at a fast food restaurant. I only remember this because I could always expect him to bring home a new kids' meal toy each week for me. My mom worked at that time in a local factory making computers.

Once, when I was five-years-old, they were in a heated argument and Dad was gathering his things and heading out to a car waiting for him at the curb in front of the house. My mother was yelling at him as he rushed out to the car, grabbing his leather jacket on the way out. The screen door crashed behind him. I ran out to him. I didn't understand what was going on, but I understood enough to know that he was leaving and that I didn't want him to go without me.

"Daddy, don't leave. Can I go with you? Please?" I stood at the curb, looking into his car full of friends, awaiting an answer.

"No," he said. "Go on back in the house." He closed the door behind him. I watched him pull off until I couldn't see the car anymore. I ran back inside.

"Mama," I said worriedly. "Where is Daddy going?"

"That's not your real daddy," she said. She turned away toward the kitchen to light a cigarette. I just stood there, stunned. I was confused but still wanted him to be my dad and I was worried that he wouldn't come back.

He did eventually return to live with us for a few more years before they broke up for good. During this time, my brother was born. After a while, I noticed a change in the adults who were raising me. While I was accustomed to them smoking cigarettes, they had taken to smoking with the doors closed. Sometimes they were alone, sometimes they were with friends. They would play cards, drink beer and alcohol, and smoke in the dining room. They would light incense of various kinds to cover up the smell of smoke. After a while, I noticed that their smoke smelled different, almost like the smell of burning plastic, a smell widely associated with smoking crack. As a child, these things seemed unimportant. I wouldn't have known about drugs at that time. I only knew they were hiding something from me, presumably grown up things that children didn't need to know about.

This was during the early 1990s, which also marked the beginning of the crack epidemic in Black neighborhoods across America. Our poor and working-class neighborhood saw a sharp increase in crime, such as breaking and entering to steal televisions and small electronics, stealing stereos out of cars and such. Children's bikes began disappearing from front yards. In addition, adults became nervous about kids playing outside too much or too far from home. In the span of just one year, our neighborhood became a place that no longer held the safety we'd previously known.

I wish I could remember more from this period in my life because this was the beginning of my mother's addiction to crack cocaine, a battle that would last for years, even decades.

Lost in Thought

My mother had her own struggles but she was adamant about one thing; she made sure I understood the importance of education and that I had what I needed to pursue it. When I was in elementary school, one of my teachers told her I was very smart and recommended a school for academically gifted and talented children. My mother did everything necessary to get me enrolled. It was good for me to be in a small setting where the teachers could understand each kid's differences and had the ability to adjust the materials. They expected a lot out of us and we performed to their expectations. I remember being engaged and challenged in that environment. I really believe attending this school gave me something to focus on to keep my mind occupied.

I was very independent as a student. The assignments I received from school awakened a desire to find answers to difficult questions. I spent a lot time looking for answers on my own and reading any and everything I could get my hands on. After a while, my aunt decided it was time to take me to the library to keep me geared toward reading books, and probably to stop me from reading everything else. It was by reading books that I realized there was a whole world out there, bigger than what I could see at the moment, and I knew in my heart that more was waiting for me.

I struggled with sadness and a sense of not having any direction. I often wondered about where my father was and why he'd left me.

Even still, I struggled with sadness and a sense of not having any direction. I often wondered about where my father was and why he'd left me. My father's relatives would come around and even bring me gifts, but he never came. Even though my mother made sure we had a roof over our heads and our needs were always taken care of, it always seemed that there was never enough money or time to do things together as a family. I spent a lot of time with other family members. When my mother left for rehabilitation for her addiction, I slipped into a cloud of darkness because my worst fears had been realized. I'd lost the only parent I had and at that moment, I felt completely abandoned. I struggled with loneliness even after she returned.

A Road and a River

The only person who ever talked about Jesus in our family was my grandmother. For a long time, I thought of church as a place where grandparents went and children only visited on Easter. Imagine my surprise when two girls invited the whole neighborhood to go to church with them. They were sisters and had only recently moved into the neighborhood and everyone seemed to like them. There was something about them that drew people and it had nothing to do with what they had. It was the first time I remember being intrigued by people who were happy for what seemed like no reason at all. At first, I didn't want to go. But when my best friend started boarding the church bus to go to church and came back telling me about it, it was enough to prompt me to go see for myself.

As it would turn out, the church I visited was small, but for some reason had a lot of young people around my age who went there regularly. Many of them were like me in that they didn't attend with parents and rode the church bus. It wasn't that the material was specifically geared toward the youth. In fact, this church was very traditional and sang songs out of hymn books for praise and worship. There were a small group of ministers who ran the service and had been attending that church since they were young. They simply taught us what was in the Bible and that was enough to keep us coming back.

It was in this church that I was taught about having a Father in heaven who saw everything we did and cared about us. Having been without my natural father in my life, this was life-changing information. I had always felt bad about my father not being there. When I was growing up, I didn't know anything about his fragile mental state. I just knew he was absent. He wasn't there to witness good moments nor was he around when I desperately needed someone to talk to. When I found out that he had another family that he supported and other children who he did pay attention to and care for, I was devastated and felt there was something wrong with me. When I found out that God was a Father of the fatherless it was good news to me.

I also learned about what sin was and that no matter how good we tried to be, we were all going to fall short without accepting Jesus Christ as our savior. They introduced me to the concept of eternity and that there was a heaven and a hell and only those who lived right before God would go to heaven.

I realized for the first time that God had a plan for my life. I'd always considered myself an accident because I knew in my heart that I was not brought into the world in a planned pregnancy. I remember asking my mother whether she had wanted to have me because once I realized the conditions I was born under, I instinctively knew that no one decided to bring me into the world. As such, I always felt like I needed to be good and stay out of trouble because I was lucky to be here and that my mother did not end my life before it began. My mother never gave me this idea; it was all in my mind. When I asked her whether she'd wanted to have me, she held me close and said, "Yes, I wanted you. I always wanted a beautiful daughter and that is exactly what I got." She told me that when she was pregnant with me, she became sick and the doctors had been afraid that she would lose me. She said she prayed and said God spoke to her heart and told her that she needed to do everything she could to make sure I was healthy and that I was going to be a unique child. Even after hearing this from my mother, I still did not believe there was any kind of intention for my life until I heard what the Bible had to say about it.

Before I formed you in the womb I knew you; before you were born I sanctified you. Jeremiah 1:5

The very idea that God could know us before we existed and that He himself shapes us helped me to see that I was here on Earth for a reason. *For I know the thoughts that I think toward you, says the Lord, thoughts of peace and not of evil, to give you a future and a hope.* Jeremiah 29:10

I realized for the first time that God had a plan for my life.

When I heard this, I understood that God cared enough about me to think good thoughts about me and that He had a future for me. I asked God to give me His thoughts toward me. My own thoughts had been so negative and had caused me to lose hope in the future.

The most powerful revelation that I received from accepting Jesus Christ as my personal savior was the promise that He would never leave or forsake us. That no matter what happened in my life, I would not be alone. Loneliness had been my struggle for such a long time. For the first time in my life, I understood that I had a guide and that the Spirit of Truth would make me free. I no longer felt the need to seek acceptance and look for people, even my parents, to validate my existence. God himself would lead me into the truth about who I was and His plan for my life. At the age of 13, I stood up in church and told God, "Send me, I'll go."

The Outcome

My life after accepting Jesus Christ as my savior has not been perfect. It has been full of many highs and lows, but I have an assurance that I did not have before. As long as I walk in truth, everything will be all right. Through God's provision and guidance, I went on to become the first person in my immediate family to graduate from college. God has blessed me beyond what I could see for myself when I gave my life to Him all those years ago.

Through my relationship with God, I have learned to see my father differently and have learned to forgive him. When I went off to college, I wrote him a letter telling him I forgave him and saying that I would like to get to know my other siblings if there was an opportunity to do that. He didn't respond, but I know it was worth it to let him know that he was forgiven and that I was praying for him. If he ever decides he wants to be in my life, I am here and willing to allow it. It is never too late to make amends.

My mother and I have a close relationship now. After many years of battling drug addiction, she conquered it in recent years and has even quit smoking cigarettes. When she married my stepfather, I gained another supporter in him. My mother is finding a new life and a renewed sense of purpose. She is able to spend quality time with her grandchildren and in many ways, is making up for lost time. The relationship we have now is exactly what I prayed for in my youth. Although it took a long time to see the outcome, it was worth waiting for.

God restored my sense of purpose, gave me a future worth living and has even restored my mother to sobriety. Even though I have yet to see my father be set free, being able to see him the way God sees him gives me hope that my prayers for him will be answered one day.

Endnotes:
Isaiah 46:19 (NKJV)
Jeremiah 1:5 (NKJV)
Jeremiah 29:10 (NKJV)

Sabrinna Stennette

Sabrinna Stennette is a playwright, contributing author in two books: *A Peace of Me; My Journey of Authenticity* and *A Glimpse of Glory*, as well as a community activist. A native of Indianapolis, IN, she obtained her degree in Organizational Leadership from Purdue University and Masters of Business Administration from Indiana Wesleyan University.

Sabrinna is the mother of Andre Stennette-Harrod, a Ball State student who was gunned down violently on Father's Day, June 17, 2012. As a surviving parent, she looks at herself as victorious, not a victim. Having found her voice, Sabrinna speaks out in the community against violence, promoting positive programs through her son's nonprofit organization, Play It 4Ward Sports and Entertainment Co.

Sabrinna also keeps her son's legacy alive though other platforms such as hosting "Syndicated Village" radio show on Dejoi Soul Café (www.dejisoul.com) and participates on panel discussions addressing violence in her community. She is a member of the Community Response Team (CRT) for the Mayor's office.

Sabrinna is a member of New Life Worship Center where she serves on the altar workers and dance ministries. She is also a member of Delta Sigma Theta Sorority, Inc. Sabrinna's foundational life scriptures are Psalms 23, Jeremiah 29:11 and Romans 8:28 and she has adopted her son Andre's motto for life, "Turn down for what?"

CHAPTER NINE

Change Me

It is in those quiet times when I'm driving in my car that God speaks to me. I remember I was driving to the meeting for the authors of this book, and while I was driving I asked God, "Why am I doing this?" I have already been a contributing author in two books, *A Peace of Me* and *A Glimpse of Glory*. I really don't have anything else to give or say. It was at that very moment Pamela Mann's song, "Change Me" came on, and God began to speak to my spirit.

He brought back the story of the eagle that my Pastor, John F. Ramsey, often tells. In this story, it mentions that an eagle can live up to 70 years. But in order to reach this age, in its 40th year it has to make a hard decision. At this age, the long and flexible talons can no longer grab prey which serves as food. It's long and sharp beak becomes bent and the feathers become old, thick, and heavy, making it difficult to fly. Then, the eagle is left with only two options: die or go through a painful process of change. During the process of change the eagle is required to fly to a mountain top and sit on its nest. The eagle knocks its beak against a rock until he breaks it off. Once the eagle's new beak grows back it has to pull out its talons. And when its new talons grow back, the eagle must pluck its old feathers and allow new ones to grow. Once the eagle has transitioned to its new body it takes its famous flight of rebirth and lives for 30 more years.

It hit me; I was going through a similar process. I began to cry and praise Him to the point my vision was blurry, because through that illustration, God reminded me that I still had untapped purpose. He also reminded me that on numerous occasions He revealed the plan He has for me. Time and time again, my response was either to ignore Him or run. I had a decision to make. Do I die with my purpose unfulfilled or do I say yes to change? By the time I reached my meeting destination, I had given the Lord my answer, "Yes, change me."

The Power of "Yes"

Yes is a powerful word. Webster defines the word yes as an affirmative answer, a decision or consent.[1]

Change is uncomfortable. It pushes us beyond our limitations. It requires total submission from us. And just like the eagle, God gives us free will. Once we say yes, God begins his work in us. When we consent to God we are giving him free rein over our lives and form merger or partnership with Him. As we partner with God, He is always at work in us.

For we are His creation - created in Christ Jesus for good works, which God prepared ahead of time so that we should walk in them (Eph. 2:10).[2]

God works in us before he can work through us. As he works on changing us he begins to take us through a similar process just like the eagle: beak breaking, talon pulling, and feather plucking.

Beak Breaking Change

The eagle has a very large, hooked beak that is used for ripping flesh from its prey and is typically heavier than that of most other birds of prey. However, at some point in the eagle's life, he comes to a proverbial crossroad between past and present where he has to decide if he is willing to change or stay the same. If he stays the same he will surely die, but if he is willing to endure the pain of getting rid of the old beak, a new one grows back bigger and stronger.

My flesh wanted to stay right there on that floor and wallow in my pain. But the Master heard my cry and suddenly I felt him wrap His loving arms around me

At some point in everyone's lives we experience a beak breaking moment. It's that pivotal decision-making moment that can set off the chain of change. It is when we get to that fork in the road of life and we have to choose if we are going to move forward and get what God has for us, or stay stuck and never actualizing God's perfect plan for us.

My beak breaking moment was on Father's Day, June 17, 2012 when I was told that my son had been murdered. I was standing in a place that no one wants to be; and far too many families stand with me. My legacy was cut off because of someone else's hostility and stupidity. I remember feeling like something inside of me had just shattered. Tears were streaming down my face and I remember calling on the name of Jesus and falling to the floor. Right there on the floor, lying prostrate, is where God found me: broken, devastated, scared, alone, empty, and confused. My flesh wanted to stay right there on that floor and wallow in my pain. But the Master heard my cry and suddenly I felt him wrap His loving arms around me and I began to release my pain through faith.[5]

Within 30 minutes of finding out that my son was dead; the news was at my door asking for an interview. I was fresh in my pain, but even at that time God required me to make a choice. I had to choose between giving in to my pain or trust God to get me through. I remember looking into the camera and with one tear rolling down my face and I said, "I forgive whoever killed my son."[5] It was at that moment of forgiveness that my beak broke and God began to manifest a new thing in me. He began to change me from the inside out and heal my broken pieces.

It is inevitable that as Christians we have gone through or will go through something that will change us in a way that we could never go back to the person we once were, but if we are willing to step out on faith, God will change us and position us to proper.

Talon Pulling Change

As a child, I was very dramatic when it came to seeing cuts, bruises, blood or anything of the sort. I remember one day my sister and I were playing in the car. Our mother had told us repeatedly to stop playing in the car before someone gets hurt. My sister and I looked at each other and ran outside and started playing in the car anyway. We were not 10 minutes into playing and I was outside screaming my head off because my sister had just slammed my fingers in the car. When I pulled my hand out of the door, one of my finger nails was injured so bad that it was hanging off by a piece of skin. Needless to say, I cut the fool. I started hollering, crying, screaming, praying, and moaning all while rolling in the grass. When we went to the doctor's office all I can remember him saying was he would have to pull the nail off because it was too damaged, but that a new nail would grow in. That is when I hit the splits. Everybody in that office heard my mouth. It took 30 minutes before I would even let the doctor touch me and another 40 minutes for me to stop crying after the nail was pulled off. It took about a month, but a new nail grew in and it was thicker and stronger than the previous nail.

I tell this story because often times as Christians we make bad choices and we don't want to be obedient to God because we don't like what He has called us to do. But even when we inflict pain on ourselves, God still favors and restores us. God is looking for some *ride or die* Christians who are willing to do whatever it takes to be more like Him.

Just think, eagles are willing to pull their powerful talons off one by one if they can no longer use them to gather food and balance themselves. I can only image the fortitude it takes to be willing to endure the pain of the process. But the eagle knows that his pain has a purpose and if he is willing to endure to the end, stronger talons will grow back and he will have new life.

If we can find within ourselves that talon-pulling faith that allows us to pluck away anything that is not of God whether it be your family, friends, job, or anything else that prevents you from living our lives Christ-like, we can begin to reposition ourselves to prosper.

God's word is used to feed and balance our spirit. As Christians, we know that God's number one purpose in life is to make us like Jesus Christ. The Spirit of God uses the Word of God to make the child of God more like the Son of God.**2** He wants us to chase after Him and hunger for His word because His word is our spiritual food. He wants us to be willing to do whatever it takes to stretch ourselves so that he can continue to pour into us.

And no one pours new wine into old wineskins. If he does, the new wine will burst the skins, the wine will run out and the wineskins will be ruined. Luke 5:37

I thank God for using me in ministry. I have been blessed to be a part of the altar workers ministry at church. This ministry pushes me to pray and fast unselfishly because we are interceding in prayer on behalf of others. And over time, without me realizing it, God has changed me. Not only do I want people to see the God in me in church, but also at my job and in my community. I find myself choosing my behavior intentionally so that I am a great representative of God no matter where I am. We have to be willing to change so that God can take us to new levels and we can grow closer to him spiritually.

Feather Plucking Change

A bird's feathers suffer regular wear and tear so; ultimately, the quality of the feather decreases and needs replaced. The loss of the feathers leaves the bird unprotected from natural elements and more importantly, it is unable to fly. Eagles need to fly in order to hunt and survive, so the loss of flight would most likely mean starvation for the bird.[3]

So often in life we as Christians weigh ourselves down with the troubles of life. We allow every circumstance to keep us from our promise. The circumstances are the problems, pressures, heartaches, difficulties, and stresses of life.

Suffering gets our attention. C. S. Lewis said that "God whispers to us in our pleasure, but shouts to us in our pain." If we are willing to change and do away with the things of life that weigh us down (pluck our feathers) then the painful circumstances - whether we bring them on ourselves, or other people cause them or the Devil incites them - are used by God to help us grow in likeness to his son.[2]

I can remember not too long ago I allowed fear to weigh me down. I couldn't remember a time in my life when it didn't frighten me to let my light shine. No matter how qualified I was I would never take a role that would bring attention to myself because I didn't want people to notice me. Fear made me insecure and lack self-worth. I was embarrassed when people complimented me so I hid behind glasses and weight. I wanted to be a public speaker but fear had me so paralyzed that I couldn't even get my thoughts together. I wanted to be a college professor, but fear had me feeling like I wasn't smart enough. Every day I came home to find my fear on my couch chillaxing in front of the big screen TV watching the football game. It had no intentions of leaving because I allowed fear of situations and things to be front and center in every aspect of my life.

I couldn't tell you the countless times I allowed fear to come back into my life and each time it stayed longer than I intended. I walked around looking okay on the outside by smiling, laughing, and faking it on the inside. When I began to unravel myself from fear's ugly web, I was completely confused and lost. I realized that fear wasn't making me happy, it was making me numb.[4]

Once I was willing to pluck the proverbial feathers of fear, I was able to find the strength to change by believing that God has given me a purpose, an assignment before I was even born.

I was able to find the strength to change by believing that God has given me a purpose, an assignment before I was even born.

For I know the plans I have for you, declares the LORD, plans to prosper you and not to harm you, plans to give you hope and a future (Jeremiah 29:11 NIV).

It is my obligation as a Christian to walk in God's purpose and plan.

We all have to start the change process. Like the eagle, we also must pluck our unpleasant memories, negative habits, and fixed mindset. Don't ever be afraid of change. Always remember God will never take anything away from you without the intention of replacing it with something much better. Only freed from past burdens can we take advantage of the present. In order to take a new journey ahead in the future, let go of your negative old, limiting beliefs, open up your fixed mindset. To truly live a Christ-like life, we must order our lives around those activities, disciplines, and practices that were modeled by Christ. The disciplines of prayer, solitude, worship, giving, tithing, serving, and others are essential to accomplish the life change that we desire.[2]

Working for My Good

God is so amazing and I will never forget what he has done for me. I began to see that even before I said yes, God was already working behind the scenes on my behalf. Many of us don't understand why things happen in our lives. Some of us in the past have had some very negative and extremely hurtful things happen to us, leaving us wondering why would a God who is so just, loving, and kind allow such a thing to happen. But understand now that God has a divine plan.[6]

We know all things God works for the good of those who love him, who have been called according to his purpose. Romans 8:28 NIV

When I look back over my life, I find that every heartache, pain, and circumstance worked together for my good because God is intentional, even when I was running, hiding, and backsliding. All of the breaking, pulling, and plucking orchestrated my life so I would be exactly in the place God wanted me to be: exposed, vulnerable, and willing for change.

Never Stop Changing

Change is continuous. When you allow yourself to change into what God has always intended you to be, not only will you position yourself to prosper, but people will begin to see Him in the way you walk and talk. You will move and speak intentionally. As Christians, we should look at change as another opportunity to be obedient and to grow. God is calling for His people to not settle for being good when they are destined for greatness. We should all be like the eagle, willing to go through the pain of change so that we can get to that next level and live out God's purpose for us. That is when we can open up ourselves and soar.

I've discovered that I am a God chaser now because I am so in love with Him. Now, during those quite times when I am driving, my prayers are so much more intimate and intentional because I want an awesome relationship with Him. I image myself sitting at God's feet and using my hair to wash His feet with my tears. All I can do is bow my head in reverence to Him and thank Him for all He has done, doing, and going to do in my life. I find myself asking God for those eagle experiences and wanting him to change me. I know that when I give it over to him and get through to the other side I will be ready for his next level. And I know He has positioned me to prosper.

A Prayer for Change

Lord we come to you first asking for forgiveness for all of our sins. We want to say thank you because Your word never comes back void. We ask that you change our hearts, minds, and spirits so that we may be worthy of the plan you have for our lives. Cleanse us of whatever is not like you so that we can be more like you every day. We boldly say yes to your will and your way. We pray for eagle experiences that will give us the fortitude to press through our pain to get to our purpose. We want to live everyday of our lives in purpose and on purpose. We are striving to be who You have authentically called us to be. Through our willingness to change, You have positioned us to proper and so the enemy is busy.

We ask that you be a hedge of protection all around us. Allow your grace and mercy to fill us with your peace and joy so even when the enemy comes to attack us all the world will see is your glory.

Amen

Endnotes:

1. www.websterdictionary.com
2. www.lifeway.com/Article/sermon-change-spiritual-growth-transformation-philippians-2
3. www.snopes.com/critters/wild/eaglerebirth.asp
4. Contributing Author Sabrinna Stennette *A Glimpse of Glory,* Chapter 10
5. Contributing Author Sabrinna Stennette *A Peace of Me,* Chapter 1
6. Pastor Martin C. Palmer www.fbhchurch.org/sermon_mcpalmer.html

Karenina Terry

Karenina Terry is a single mother of two beautiful girls and assists with raising her oldest nephew. Karenina loves her family and friends. One of her favorite things to do is to cook a big meal to show her love for them. In her downtime, she curls up with a good book and listens to music of all genres. She also enjoys romantic comedies and fantasy movies. She is an advocate for continuing education.

After graduating high school, Karenina enrolled in cosmetology school. She became a licensed hair stylist. She is now realizing her dream by pursuing her passion to counsel families in strengthening their relationship/love life. She received a full scholarship to Ivy Tech where she is studying for her associates in liberal arts. She then hopes to transfer to IUPUI in the Fall of 2018 to major in psychology. Karenina is active in her local church as a praise dancer and choir member. She also helps out in the church office and will soon be leading the young adult ministry.

Karenina currently works as a medical billing representative. Her desire is to complete her book encouraging women to be free from their past in the near future. She is grateful for this, the first of many opportunities on the horizon for her and her family.

CHAPTER TEN

Let It Go

And we know that ALL things work together for the good to them that love God, to them who are called according to his purpose. Romans 8:28 KJV

We all are born with a purpose. No matter how we arrived on the planet, we are no accident. It is up to us to discover who we are to pursue our destiny and live out our purpose. Why doesn't that happen? I can't answer that, but I am convinced there is an enemy to our destiny. He is on assignment to kill, steal, and destroy. I have faced many roadblocks trying to find me. I have believed lies about love. I've been through the good, the bad, and the ugly to get to where I am now. Have I arrived? Not fully. Every day my eyes open and my feet hit the floor, I am "Positioned to Prosper." I share my story in hopes it will help you on your way to fulfilling your purpose.

Why Don't You Love Me?

The little girl in me has been wounded for a long time. It has taken a few years for the woman to recognize the little girl needed to be healed in order for the woman to continue to grow. I was stuck. Nothing seemed to be working for me. Why?

There was something in my past hindering me from progressing in my present and future. I had to find out what that was and deal with it. So my story begins with a man. Surprised? Probably not, that seems to be the starting point for most of our healing.

Growing up I was surrounded by plenty of people that loved me. I lived with my grandma, mother, and twin brothers; and there were plenty of other family members around. My father was present when he could be.

The absence of my father saddened me. His mother played a very significant role in my life. She kept me connected to my father. Her presence in my life helped to pacify the void when he wasn't around.

Now here I am, an adult. As I said before, I grew up surrounded by people who loved. But the one person I needed to love me wasn't there. When I was about six years old, I remember my father having a conversation with me over the phone informing me that he would be moving out of state. At that age I wasn't really interested in why he was moving, all I knew was that he was leaving me. "You know Daddy loves you right?" That's all he kept saying, and I would respond "yes" but my heart felt different. If you love me, then why are you leaving me?

Lie #1: Men who love you will always leave you and come back and leave again and it's okay.

He ended up moving to California. The next time I saw him was during one of my summer visits with my grandmother. He arrived with a wife and child. I was ecstatic to have a new sister. After a few days he was gone again. I would not see him for three years.

When he moved back home, I was a teenager and doing the teenage thing. We talked every now and again. Then, during my last two years of high school, things changed. I remember him being at all my special events; prom, graduation, and he even bought my first car. It is during this time that I lost a few friends to senseless violence and learned my dad was terminally ill. He was diagnosed with HIV.

I spent the next few years helping his wife and my grandmother care for him. I didn't know how much time we had left, and I wanted to be daddy's girl for whatever time we had left. When his vision started to fail, I would sit with him. We would talk and laugh about the things going on in our lives. One of the things going on in my life was I had met a man. Things between us weren't that great and I was thinking about breaking up with him. But for that moment I had the two things I thought I wanted most, two men who I hoped loved me.

One day during our visit I looked at my dad and asked him, "Do you REALLY love me?" I believe it caught him off guard.

After a brief silence, I saw a tear roll down his cheek. My father turned to me and said, "Of course I, I always have. I just went through some things in life that didn't allow me to love you the way you deserved to be loved, so I stayed away."

Finally, I heard it. My father loved me. I didn't fully understand his answer but a light bulb went off. My propensity for unhealthy relationships stemmed from me looking for love from people who weren't capable of loving me.

My father was hospitalized. I was told that he probably would not make it back home. I was not prepared for what I might have to face. It took me all day to get up the nerve to go to the hospital. When I got there he was hooked up to several machines. The pneumonia was winning this battle. He was on oxygen. I sat beside him and held his hand. It was cold. I remembered back to my aunt's body being cold before she passed.

I was not ready for my father to leave me. Our relationship was not perfect, but at least we did have one. I sat and talked to him for a while and got up to move to the other side of the bed. The strangest thing happened. I noticed he was following me with his eyes. When I got to the other side, he smiled and said, "Do you forgive me?"

I told him "yes."

He then said, "I love you little lady, always have, always will." I told him I loved him and I would see him the next day, he just smiled. He knew that moment would be our last.

My father died that night. I received the call as soon as I walked in the door. His wife told me he passed away right after I left. I went through a range of emotions. I was glad he was out of pain. I was angry that he left just as we were developing the relationship I desired. I was thankful for the relationship we did have. Now it was over. He would continue to be in my heart and I would continue to be in this relationship I wasn't sure about.

Lie #2: Men who love you can't always love you back the way you deserve to be loved and you have to accept it.

Blinded by the Thought of Love

Sometimes we just need to listen to our elders. I have learned that our mothers and grandmothers really do always know what they are talking about. I wish I had learned this lesson earlier, it would have prevented some hard knocks.

I wish I had learned this lesson earlier, it would have prevented some hard knocks.

My grandmother told me before I got involved with the man, "You better watch that boy; he's a little too clingy for my liking." I thought it was cute and sweet that he called often to "check on me." He delivered to the company where I worked. Let's call him Mr. Xerox. He would come to the back of the building where he knew I would be making copies. His flirtatious way of smiling and speaking to me, not to mention, the swag made me smile back with a sultry hello. One day he asked me to go to lunch. I didn't see any harm, since everyone knew where I was and his job was attached to the company, so I went. It was a good lunch. We talked, laughed, and exchanged numbers. We talked all the time after that.

I really should have listened to Grandma and left him alone then. Or definitely after the first time he hit me, leaving a gash across my nose. I didn't leave then. I didn't leave the next time or the next. I stayed with him for eight years. Eight years I suffered through him cheating on me, hitting on me, and verbally/emotionally abusing me.

During this time I conceived our daughter. It was a difficult pregnancy and I was put on bed rest due to my blood pressure. He insisted on acting a fool at the hospital. I later learned that he had gotten another girl pregnant at the same time and took his frustration out on me. Our daughter was born at thirty-two weeks, weighing 2-pounds and 15- ounces. Low birth weight was the only concern. God's grace and mercy was shown to us that day, but we did not recognize it.

I had finally had enough two years after our daughter was born. We separated for about a year, but he kept in touch with his daughter. One evening I received a call from him informing me his grandmother had passed away and asking if I could be there with him for support. I took our daughter and even stayed a little while after. After everything was over he asked if I could bring our daughter to his place and I did.

Three months later I found out I was pregnant again. I was very disappointed in myself because I always knew I wanted to be married before I had another child, I just didn't want to be married to him. So why did I stay? He loved me and wanted to be with me? No, the abuse continued.

Our second daughter was born in August of 2006. What joy my children have always given me. They are what held me together. It wasn't until his actions threatened to hurt my babies that I gained to courage to get out of this relationship. During an altercation, while holding the baby and our oldest by my side, I caught a glimpse of a hair brush flying past my face. His sister came and got him that night at my request. He was gone, but his harassment, threats, and verbal abuse continued for months. I remember some of his last words to me; "Don't nobody want you." Those words stuck to me like glue and I believed them.

Lie #3: Men who love you abuse you because they are afraid of losing you to someone else and you have to live with it.

The Love of Family

Looking back at this next relationship makes me wonder where my head was. At a party one night, in walks this man I was kind of acquainted with. Let's call him Mr. Smooth. We talked, we laughed, and we connected. I wasn't sure if my spirit connected to him or my flesh.

Flesh won that round. That night started an "it is what it is" relationship. We would hook up and go on doing our own thing. Then he suddenly disappeared. Can't really explain how I felt about his disappearing act, but I had to honor the "it is what it is" and accept "now it isn't."

One day out of the blue, a mutual friend informed me that Mr. Smooth was looking for me. At first I wasn't interested. My curiosity finally got the best of me. I wanted answers.

I found out he had a son. We got back together. Slow at first, but I had an uneasy feeling. I felt our relationship was a secret. When asked why, he said, "To keep down confusion." Being a father and spending time with his son was important to him, which is something I respected, I went along with it. He started to bring his son around me. We were doing things as a family. I was now not only in love with him, I was in love with his son as well.

Lie #4: Men who love you will never fully commit to you.

I finally had the family I wanted. We loved each other. Our children were being raised as siblings. I would do anything to protect what we had. Sometimes in relationships we open doors, giving the enemy more access and permission to steal, kill, and destroy. The crazy part is you never know how or when he's going him to come in. Needless to say, I wasn't prepared.

God will show up just when you need him to. It was like someone rolled the stone away from the dark tomb I was in and called my name!

Mr. Smooth started drinking more, staying out later and every form of abuse/disrespect increased. There was no trust. He openly cheated on me. He was frustrated and he took his frustration out on me. We had shouting matches on a regular basis. Some led to physical altercations. I knew his behavior was unacceptable, but I always made excuses for him. He told me I was the dumbest woman he had ever dealt with. You know, he was right in a sense. I still stayed. This was my family and I would do anything to protect it.

To escape what was going on around me, I lost myself in reading and social media. It was fun interacting with different people. I could be whoever I wanted to be. My fun and escape led to a relationship with a man I met on social media. Let's call him Mr. Internet. He was everything I thought I ever wanted. He was all about me. I blew him off, still hoping my relationship with my boyfriend would get back on track. I didn't realize that I had established an emotional bond with Mr. Internet. Talking with him, sharing my feelings and desires, letting him into my soul, had created a bond between us. He was kind, attentive, and willing to be the man I desired. He was everything I needed at that time. I moved away from Mr. Smooth and started seeing Mr. Internet. He was good to me. He was too good to me. I started feeling guilty. I started feeling like I didn't deserve to be treated this way. I wasn't good enough to be loved by him. I didn't feel worthy of this man's affection. I didn't believe this was real.

Meanwhile, Mr. Smooth was trying to get back with me. He had nothing to offer me but he was who I wanted to be with. He represented family to me. He represented the only type of love I knew. I went back to him. I destroyed a relationship that possibly could have been sent to me by God to go back and forth with an individual that had no idea how to love me.

Lie #5: You don't deserve to be loved (the biggest one of all!)

Love under New Management

My view of love was tainted from childhood. I believed the lies of the enemy that were sent to destroy my destiny. I lived in the shadow of those lies for a long time. Then it happened. The truth caught up with me. On March 8, 2015 during an evening service, my pastor called me out and began talking to me about what was going on in my life. My pastor didn't know me like that...he didn't know my business so I knew it was God telling me, "Enough is Enough! You gotta let it go!"

You see, God will show up just when you need him to. It was like someone rolled the stone away from the dark tomb I was in and called my name! The blinders fell from my eyes and I could see clearly.

All these years I thought I was being guided by love. It was the lust of my flesh. My spirit was broken and empty. I looked for love from my father and several other men. I believed the lie that what they were giving me was love. I did not know love because I did not know God. God is love. I could not give love because I did not love myself.

For the past two years I have been developing a love relationship with God. Jesus is now the Lover of My Soul. I am learning a lot about myself. Some good, some bad, but all designed to make me better. I am learning how to "Let it Go." I am learning to forgive others and myself. I am learning how to recognize God in all things. I am learning how to love me! That is so exciting to me! I can now live with purpose and love on purpose because I trust God in all things.

WHEN YOU DON'T LOVE YOURSELF, YOU EXPECT PEOPLE TO FILL THAT VOID...LOVING YOURSELF OPENS YOUR EYES TO THE REALITY OF YOUR SITUATION

Listen, wherever you are in life, it is not too late. Right where you are is your starting point. You have not made too many mistakes. Look for the signs God is putting in your path and follow them. Keep your eyes and ears open. Stay ready. Keep it moving. Let go of past hurt. Forgive those that have hurt you. Forgive you for hurting you. Not everyone you love will stay…let them go. Not everyone you trust will be loyal…guard your heart. Some people only exist as examples of what to avoid…BE AWARE. Let go of regret. Learn from your past. Don't be controlled by it. Let it Go! Let it Go! Let it Go! And LIVE!

Stacia D. Washington

Stacia D. Washington has a dynamic testimony and message that has captured many hearts and encouraged lost souls. She is a native of Indianapolis, IN, and is a *Virtuous Woman* of God who enjoys working in the vineyard. Stacia's inspiration comes from her southern roots, raising a child as a single parent, and modeling her life around Proverbs 31. While living in Indy, she was very active in church. Stacia served as a Girl Scout troop leader and community activist who has campaigned for various politicians.

Stacia was a prominent figure and motivational speaker within the faith-based community during former President Barack Obama's presidential campaign. As a community organizer, she was not only successful in orchestrating efforts for voter's registration in Indiana, but also assisting in efforts to maintain the Illinois – Indiana Ministers Alliance under the leadership of the late Bishop James E. Tyson, in which she received the Outstanding Community Organizer Award.

With the grace of God, she has survived many challenges in life that some would deem as unbelievable. Her response is, "God allowed me to go through in order to mold me into the *Virtuous Woman* I am today and share my testimony with others on being *Positioned To Prosper*."

Today, this author resides in Nashville, Tennessee where she humbly serves within her church and community. Stay tuned to see what comes next from Stacia D. Washington.

CHAPTER ELEVEN

When God Is Positioning You... Follow Directions

Have you ever questioned God about your purpose in life? Do you ask why bad things happen to good people? Has God ever brought you out of a dark place? Well, you are not alone because I think most Christians (if they are honest) would answer 'Yes' to all the above. It is not by chance you are reading this chapter. I firmly believe that God is allowing me to share my testimony so that you will be able to keep the faith and know that God is positioning you for greatness. Be patient, wait on the Lord, and learn from your mistakes.

God Is Strategically Positioning Me...He Is My Compass

I know that God has a purpose for me and a divine calling upon my life. Instantly, when some people hear this, they automatically assume that this person is trying to be in someone's pulpit or start up a store front church. But this is not the case. While some are fighting for status and a title, there are others (such as myself) who know that the real work of God is out in the vineyard. That's right. If we are to be Christ-like, we must work amongst his people and his people are out in the vineyard.

I accepted Christ at a young age and knew why I was choosing him to be my Lord and Savior. Back then, my Pastor (the late Dr. Arthur Johnson of Friendship Missionary Baptist Church in Indianapolis) was an old school pastor from Mississippi who brought the word all the way to Indy. He taught his flock well and had us out in the vineyard praying, anointing, feeding, and clothing the homeless, drug addicts, prostitutes, and you name it. As a child, I was not afraid, because after all, our pastor was with us and our church was known as the 'Ship' rocking and swaying through the neighborhoods.

That experience alone taught me how to love people for who they are and not for what they had. It showed me that even someone with the worst tattered clothes, reeking of an awful stench, could be saved and had a testimony to share.

It taught me to treat others the way you would want to be treated. And most of all, it allowed me to see that if I did not make the right choices, my life could very well end up similar to those we were ministering. When God orders our steps, there are times we will not know why he is directing our path in unfamiliar areas and places, even amongst people who are not like us.

Train up a child in the way he should go, and when he is old he will not depart far from it. Proverbs 22:6

He Is My Protector

Many years ago, my car stopped on some railroad tracks after Sunday church service. The good Samaritans driving behind me stopped, pushed my car off the tracks and gave me a ride to my parent's house down the street.

I was a little heartbroken because that was my only means of transportation and I did not know if I could afford to have a car payment.

About a week later, my father and I went to a car dealership to look for another car for me. My first choice was a black Oldsmobile Alero with the tinted windows and booming sound system. When we tried to look underneath the hood to see the engine, I found a dead bird on the windshield. Immediately I knew that was not the car for me. After pacing up and down the many rows of cars on the outside of the dealership, my father asked me to take a look at the vehicles inside on the showroom floor. Instantly, I saw something that caught my eye, and that's when I walked up to the car of my dreams. I screeched with excitement and told everyone inside I just fell in love with a candy apple red Oldsmobile Alero.

There was a time I made the mistake of ignoring the red flags that God was trying to show me. Believe me when I say there were consequences behind that.

Let's just say it was nobody but God that allowed my application to get approved. I was in shock and afraid to drive my new car home. When I prayed and thanked God for my blessing, I also asked him a funny question...out of all colors, why the color RED? God told me that since I had been faithful in paying my tithes, he approved the deal. And, to remind me of his favor towards me, the color RED was to show I was covered with his blood. I shouted for joy!

A couple years later, I became ill and was unable to work. I couldn't make a car payment, pay other bills, and had to rely on my parents to take care of me and my daughter until I got well. Also during that time, something else happened, my car got repossessed during the week of Thanksgiving, out of all days. I was heartbroken and I cried. All I could think about was why something like this had to happen to me at this inopportune time? When it seemed like everything was going so good, why now? No matter how bad I felt, and in the midst of the storm, I did not lose faith. I remembered how Job kept his faith in God even when his wife and friends mocked him. I remembered God's promise and as painful as it was, I began to praise God in the midst of my pain.

Just a few days later, my mother (whose name is Glory) and I were on our way back home from grocery shopping when a car veered into our lane, hitting us head-on. The driver of the vehicle that hit us was cut from ear to ear and had to be rushed to the hospital. My mother and I were also taken to the hospital whereas the impact totaled the car and caused us great pain. The officer on the scene said that if we had not worn our seatbelts we would not have made it out alive.

After reading the police report, I started viewing the pictures of my mother's car after the accident. As I started saying, 'Thank You Jesus' something dawned on me and I felt a heaviness in my spirit. That is when I realized that God really did keep his promise when he said that my candy apple red Oldsmobile Alero was a reminder of him covering me with his blood. You see, at the time of the accident my car had been repossessed, which meant I could not drive it that particular day. Therefore, my mother had to drive her Bonneville (which was made out of heavier material) in turn saving our lives during the impact of the accident. To God be the Glory!

He Is My Restorer

We as Christians not only have to be careful of what we pray for, but we must be patient and not anxious for anything. There was a time I made the mistake of ignoring the red flags that God was trying to show me. Believe me when I say there were consequences behind that. The experience put me in a dark place in which I did not know what to do, how to handle it, or who to turn to. The traumatic plague has forever changed my life. It almost cost me my life. I was in shock and fell into a great depression and isolated myself. I was afraid, couldn't sleep, and wouldn't eat. I wanted to hate, but God wouldn't let me. I wanted to run, but God kept ahold of me.

I can still recall the first time I heard my pastor preach. I was still in the dark place of my life and really needed to be fed in the spirit. Within his message, Pastor made a reflection upon a story about a little girl who received rave reviews after her piano recital. He mentioned that her instructor had been interviewed and provided somewhat of a modest assessment. But what grasped my attention was when I heard why her instructor's response was so vague. Pastor said the instructor stated the pianist would be at the peak of her greatest work once she experienced tragedy. Her music will then tell a story. And, like the pianist, I had a story.

That message hit home and is still with me until this very day. I then realized that I was like the pianist, and the only difference between me and her was that tragedy had already hit. I am not ashamed to say it nor can I deny that I am a survivor of domestic violence. Now, I will not bore you with the…who, what, when, or where. Nevertheless, I will tell you how it was nobody but God who restored me.

One day, I sat down at the top of my staircase and had a talk with God. It seemed like I did all the talking and he just listened, waiting for me to finish. Like many times before, God put something in my spirit. This is when I asked God to show me where I went wrong. And, that is exactly what he did.

We as Christians not only have to be careful of what we pray for, but we must be patient and not anxious for anything.

At that moment, God revealed to me my decision-making process was not necessarily His will for my life. Even when He tried to warn me about some people, places, and things, ultimately, I decided to ignore the signs and proceed without caution. He comforted and reassured me that this too shall pass and promised to fill the void in my heart. He also ministered to me and told me that in spite of what I was feeling in the flesh, I still needed to forgive the individual for what had happened. Last but not least, God restored my faith when he reminded me that every person he called upon to work in his vineyard had a story to tell, such as David, Daniel, and Job…and this also includes the *Virtuous Woman*.

Now, don't get me wrong, I am not saying that I am blaming myself for what happened. But what I will say is that I am taking responsibility for not listening to

God and having patience to wait on the man of God that he had for me. After having that heart-to-heart conversation with the Lord, I knew that I had some work to do. I began praying and repenting until my soul got tired of praying. I started taking back everything that Satan had stolen from me. I took back my self-esteem, joy, goals, and everything else you could imagine...especially my will to live. And finally, I started working even harder in God's vineyard, using my life experiences as a testimony to help others.

He Positioned Me to Prosper

People say that life experiences will bring about a change. I have found this to be true as crazy as it may sound. As we live our everyday lives, we need not to ever forget that God has a divine purpose for our life, He allows things to happen for a reason and He is positioning us to prosper. It is up to us to follow the instructions in order to safely get to our destination. The Bible is our manual and God is our compass.

Therefore, don't give up when you come across challenges, mountains, or even a fork in the road. Remember that God is always with you and what He allows you to go through is only a test. It may seem as though He is silent when you pray, but He is still there. It may even look as though you are about to fall into the deepest pit, nevertheless He catches you just in time. You may even pray at times for God to remove the gigantic mountains; then somehow He removes you instead in order to protect you from the storms ahead. After all, He is our protector.

But then, if you should stumble and fall, allow God to be the comforter and Father that He truly is. It may hurt to hear the truth about your disobedience, but it is meant to teach you lessons about life, install nuggets of wisdom, and bring you closer to God. The one thing I love the most is knowing that in spite of what goes on in our life, He continues to love us, forgive us, and restore us. This is something that even man does not do. With all of this in mind, it is no wonder we are Positioned to Prosper.

For I know the plans I have for you," declares the Lord, "plans to prosper you and not to harm you, plans to give you hope and a future. Jeremiah 29:11 -

My Prayer for Positioning & Prospering

Dear eternal God, as I take this moment to welcome you with an open heart, mind, arms, and soul, I just want to say 'Thank-You.' Thank you, dear Lord, for you saw it in your will to wake us up out of slumber to see another glorious day that you have made. Thank you for your love, patience, goodness, and mercy. Thank you for your son who died for our sins. Thank you for another chance even though we did not deserve it. Thank you for your protection whenever we drifted off course. Thank you Lord for the mountains we had to climb that made us strong. Thank you for even the harvest of blessings that are yet to come. Lord, I can't Thank you enough!

I appreciate you giving me the courage to be transparent, allowing me to share this message with others who may need encouragement and the will to go that extra mile. I dare not take this moment for granted. I know from whom my blessings come from. Use me dear Lord as a vessel in your kingdom as you continue to expand my territory.

Please forgive us of our sins and spew out anything that is not of you. We ask that you break generational curses, un-equal yokes, and any strongholds that may be a hindrance as you continue to position us to prosper. We ask dear Lord as you replenish our souls, our minds, and hearts that you place your whole armor upon us. Anoint us from the crown of our head to the soles of our feet. Teach us to be Christ-like and love one another like Christ loves the church. Give us the spirit of discernment as you order our steps down the pathway towards righteousness.

Father, we ask that you speak to us clearly in your own divine way as to what we should do whenever we come to the fork in the road. And, as we step out on faith, Lord we ask that you pick us up and wipe the dust off if we should stumble and fall. And, when we finally get to our destination or position in life, we ask that you continue keep us humble in those high places. Allow your anointing to glow upon us where others may ask how they too can be saved and get in position to prosper...Amen!

Endnotes:
Proverbs 22:6
Jeremiah 29:11 KJV

LaTasha White

LaTasha White has a passion for caring for Gods' people, and considers it an honor. She is a wife, mother, Registered Nurse, published author, and a Certified John Maxwell leadership coach, speaker, and trainer. She has a strong gift and foundation of faith. She puts her trust in God, as He leads her through her purpose.

LaTasha and her husband, Reginald, have shared 21 years of marriage. They are the proud parents of high school sophomore, Omar; college sophomore, Zharquan, and 23-year old, Kiara, who is the mother of their first grandson, 2 yr. old, Kamari.

. Most recently she has taken the leap to become a Certified Coach through the John Maxwell Team and Human Behavior Consultant with Authentic Identify Institute. Early 2016, she and her husband launched Grow Into Victory Intentionally, LLC. At GIVIN, they specialize in self-leadership coaching through mastermind groups, one on one coaching, DISC personality assessments, and spiritual gift analysis.

In LaTasha's first book collaboration, she had the honor of being a part of through Authentic Identity Institute, *A Glimpse of Glory-Seeing God in the Midst of it All*, 2017, she writes of the transparent journey of her 20-year marriage to Reginald. She openly shares her life, so that she may not only be a testimony, but a light, for others who need lead to the throne.

CHAPTER TWELVE

From Here to There

We wait…

Yay! Saturday morning is finally here! The day we get to go spend the night with Daddy. My little brother and I are up and dressed. I've packed our little blue suitcase, we've had breakfast, Mom has done my hair with tight pigtails so Daddy doesn't have to try to mess with it. We are all ready! I perch myself on the big brown ottoman, I don't want to play while I wait because I want to stay pretty for Daddy.

My little brother is playing with his cars in the doorway, and doesn't seem to have as much anticipation as me. It's now lunch time, Mom comes into the living room, and asks if we want to eat lunch. I immediately snap back, "No, I want to be ready when Daddy comes! He will probably be here any minute so he can take us to lunch." Mom's only reply was, "Ok baby." I continue to sit there.

Little brother, Steve, asks, "Is he still coming?"

I reply, "Yep, he's just running late."

Dinner time rolls around, and it's starting to get dark. I ask Mom to call him, she says she already has and there was no answer. [Of course, back then there were no cell phones, and definitely no social media to track a person's every move.] Mom makes us dinner, at this point I give in to eating, only to immediately return to my waiting seat once I finished.

It's very dark now, it must be about 10-11p.m. Mom tells us to get our pajamas on and prepare for bed. Of course, I argue that Daddy is still coming, and I have to wait. Mom, with sad eyes, says "Baby he's not coming tonight."

I open our little blue suitcase and remove our pajamas, being sure to leave everything else intact. Reluctantly, I drag my feet to bed. Brokenhearted and wondering what I must have done to make Dad mad. He must be mad at me, otherwise he would've came, right?

Mom and Daddy got divorced when I was five and my brother Steve was just an infant. I didn't know what to expect from a family, but I knew mine was different from my friends.

This scenario repeated itself more times than I can count. What I did not know as a seven-year-old little girl was the battle with addictions Daddy was having.

He always looked and smelled good. Everyone loved him; he was the life of any room he was in. How could he possibly be drinking and using drugs? Why are people saying this? By the time I was ten, Steve was only five, we took our first family trip. We drove, for only a couple of hours, checked into a hotel, then went to a nearby building where I heard my mom say we're here for our family session. I was thinking huh? What session? What is this? What's going on? What are we doing?

I quickly found out we were to spend a few days in counseling for families of addiction. Little did I know, Daddy was there as a patient in their program.

There's hope...

I learned to recite the Serenity Prayer while we were there. *God grant me the serenity to accept the things I cannot change: courage to change the things I can: and the wisdom to know the difference.* At the time I did not understand, but as I grew up, this prayer was the very thing that got me through some very tough years that were ahead of me.

Once Daddy was released, I was completely convinced that he was fixed. I dreamed of going to do all kinds of things that my friends were doing with their dads, going to Delco park, going skating, out to restaurants, you name it, I was so excited for it. My dreams came true! Daddy would arrive to pick us up, as planned, no waiting. We'd go to dinner, and visit his friends, who also had kids that we could play with. Life was good; this was how it was supposed to be.

But all of the disappointments prior to this started building this wall that I didn't even know was being built, brick by brick. I found myself holding my breath each time we had a scheduled pick up time. As the months and years wore on, those dates got broken more and more often. You'd think it would make me angry, bitter, or even mad. Instead, I became tolerant.

The detriment of this tolerance started showing up as a teenager, especially in the dating arena. I allowed myself to be treated "any type of way" so that my boyfriends wouldn't leave.

Seriously…

Stacked on top of "dealing" with Daddy's addiction to cocaine and alcohol, when I was 12 Mom started dating. She had done so on and off, but nothing serious. Well, this one moved in. I quickly saw the same signs of addiction that my father had. I couldn't believe this. I think I was shocked that she would allow herself to go through this again. He did buy us nice things, and took my brother and I in as his own. The experience seemed different because he lived with us, while Daddy did not. What was the same was unpredictable moods and atmosphere of the house each evening. The thing I remember most was the fits of rage against neighbors, or anyone he felt wronged him. Again, my tolerance allowed me to turn the other cheek. This was my self-preservation, my protection from my own emotions.

After a few years, they married. We've always referred to him as Pops, as even then step dad seemed too harsh. We were able to witness him being delivered from the strongholds of the addictions of drugs and alcohol. Pops had begun going to church regularly, and started taking college classes, graduating with a degree in drug and alcohol counseling. Wow, this is a huge difference in the life we were used to!

I moved out of my parent's home just two months after graduating high school. This same year I met the man who would become my husband. What I found was that all of the years of tolerance had worn thin by this time; I took every bit of it out on him. Secretly my mind told me that if he really wanted me he'd stay. Always having the thought he would leave just like Daddy did. He never deserved any of the projected feelings I put on him. He wasn't the one who left. He wasn't an addict, although I treated him just like he was. I'm forever grateful for his understanding, even when I didn't know how to explain why I acted the way I did at times.

My world changed…

It was when I was in my early 20's that the anger finally rose to the surface. Daddy had passed away when I was 22, due to the alcohol abuse, he was clean of the drugs (as far as I know) for years prior to his passing, but he just could not shake the alcohol. I had no idea he was sick, well not this sick. I had started to notice he was much weaker than normal. I vividly recall him carrying our 18-month-old son down the stairs and quickly handing him off to me as he stumbled down the rest of the steps, only to collapse in the nearest chair. My Daddy was fit, not overweight at all, he loved playing racquetball with friends, and to see him weak like that was a bit alarming. All he said was, "I'm ok, I just lost my balance a little." This was only one week prior to what would end up being his last day on Earth. I'd spent much of my later teenage years avoiding the conversation with him that were always filled with set ups and let downs. I had so much resentment for him being taken away, and I never got a chance to have those conversations with him that would help me understand how to move on in life, knowing I could not pick up the phone and chat, even if I wanted to. Deep down I knew that he was better off and his struggle was

The one thing I knew for sure was that I needed to have a relationship with the Lord.

over. That did not keep me from aching, wondering, and questioning.

The one thing I knew for sure was that I needed to have a relationship with the Lord. Because his passing at 43 years old made me realize we don't have forever to get it together. Now don't get me wrong, I definitely did not always strive to serve the Lord with all of my being. I've grown into that, and I'll share more with you a little later in this chapter, but I did have the seed planted. Thankfully, God gives us grace to sort ourselves out.

Pick up the pieces...

I'm heartbroken. I realize I can't bring Daddy back, but I can make him proud. He always wanted to be sure we were doing well in school and making wise choices. Through the years of being in and out of addiction we got to see glimpses of the amazing man he was. I began to remember all of the countless Alcoholics and Narcotics Anonymous (AA/NA) meetings he'd taken me to with him, as a teenager. At the time, I didn't understand why I had to sit there, but it did help me to understand the disease he was battling, and that countless others were too. What can I do to make any of this worth it? He only wanted the best for us, and I needed to make sure I did everything in my power to keep pushing. I needed to break this cycle, to create a different legacy for our children.

I pushed to complete nursing school when it would have been easy to give in to life's curve balls. If you've read my first book collaboration *A Glimpse of Glory: Seeing God in the Midst of it All*, you know this story.

My husband was very ill and I was in my last semester of nursing school. Do I put everything on hold, or do I push? I chose to push, graduating on time. I was so proud of this accomplishment and Daddy would've been too. I could have settled for living a "normal" day to day, as a nurse, a mom, a wife. But no, the push is too great in me and the need for me to show up in this world is enormous. Through my daily quiet time with God, reading His Word, asking Him for direction, and ultimately giving Him my yes; I began to study personal growth and development, as I understood I needed to change myself. As I grew through hurt, pain, self-sabotage, and feeling like I never measured up, I had the strong pull to help other women work through their baggage and show up differently in life. I became a certified leadership coach, focusing on self-leadership as my way to help others see they hold the pen to their story. A lot happens to us, but how we react is what predicts the outcome.

Sibling perspective...

I had the privilege to interview my brother, Mom, and Pops. In the next few paragraphs you'll read a small piece of living through addiction from their vantage points. During the interview with Steve, my little brother, who I mention in the beginning of this chapter, he spoke of many life lessons he learned from, both our father and our Pops. Steve said that Daddy would give him many life lessons, especially during the time he would cut his hair for him. It seems he wanted to prepare Steve to make a better life for himself than he had. Daddy told him things like, "You either need to learn every skill you need in life, or you need to make enough money to be able to pay someone else to do it for you."

Steve says he believes this is one of the reasons he is in constant competition with himself. He adds "I always have to go harder, and do more." His word has become his bond because he'd learned at an early age what it felt like to be given someone's word only to have it broken. "If I give my word, you can bet I'm going to do it!"

Steve acknowledges that the broken promises have caused him to have trust issues, and is skeptical of everyone, until they prove themselves. "There is a lot that I have purposefully forgotten, because I never want to relive those tough days. Daddy was a cool dude and he had a certain style. The more I tried to not be like him, the more I am. I stopped fighting against it. Now that I'm 35 I even dress like him."

Steve finished up the interview with this, "If I had to give one quote to sum up what I've learned this far it would be that 'You can put your own twist on life, it doesn't have to be the script that was written.'"

Mother's perspective...

What's the lesson you've learned that you need to share with other wives and mothers about being married to someone who suffers with addiction?

"The person you met and fell in love with is not the person you'll spend the rest of your life with. You stay, you wait, you live for the sweet moments. They come, but only far and few between. What I have come to understand is that it's not the person that's bad, it's the addiction that's bad."

Mom adds she never wanted us kids to see how broken she was, therefore she never cried. It was my little brother who'd asked her why she never did because he'd seen other women cry, but never Mom. It was then that she realized how callused she'd become. "When you get this way, you're not giving or receiving love."

What I know is that we've all got a story, and it's ok. Work on how you can change your own life.

How do you think you ended up marrying two addicts? "The first time I didn't know any better. The second time, things moved too fast for me to realize it was a cycle that I needed to break."

Describe the struggle of raising children while being married to a person with addiction. "Trying to make life as normal as possible. All day everyday was an act, trying to put up a happy front. Cocaine is a predictable addiction and I could almost brace myself and prepare for the bad weekend to come once the paycheck came. The alcohol is not predictable at all, it's readily available, accessible, and socially acceptable to have a drink. The part no one sees are the several other drinks that were had when no one was looking."

What is your wisdom for wives to push through to the other side? "What I finally understood is exactly that…P.U.S.H, Pray Until Something Happens. Anoint everything your husband touches from their hair brush to their car steering wheel. Read and apply daily devotions. I know God has favor on me and he'll never let anything go too far to harm me, as long as I continue to serve Him."

Father's perspective...

I would have been remiss to wrap up this entire chapter of growth through addiction without interviewing Pops. Pops was an addict, and by the grace of God, has lived through to see the other side of the dark place called addiction.

I asked what was his biggest challenge raising a family, while battling addiction? "I wanted to beat the addiction to keep the family together, all five of you were my children and I wanted it to stay that way. I was sick and tired of being sick and tired. Chasin' Jason trying to catch up with the 'white ghost' ruined my life." This is what they referred to when looking for the next cocaine high.

What's your recommendation to other fathers currently struggling with addictions? "Seek help! Understand that you cannot do it alone. You need the 12 steps of NA and AA, plus the 10 commandments of the Bible. There will be a void when you stop the drugs and alcohol. You will fill it with something, be mindful, careful, and selective about what that is, only the Holy Spirit will do. This is reiterated in the book of Matthew 12:44."

Why do I share this story?

I have been given the grace to grow through to the other side of being a product of addiction, and I owe it to others to know and understand that this is not the end of your story. On most days, I show up in the world polished and put together, no one knows how many years I spent broken, trying to put together the pieces that nobody saw. What I know is that we've all got a story, and it's ok. Work on how you can change your own life. You absolutely cannot change anyone else. The world will respond to how you treat yourself. Understand that the journey is not easy, but worth it. When you feel comfortable in your skin, and not like you're pushing against the world every single day to understand how you fit, it will all begin to make sense. Our lives are a huge puzzle. Every battle and victory is another piece to that.

The biggest game changer is developing a relationship with our Heavenly Father. We are merely spinning our wheels, until we tap into the true purpose He has for us. I am telling you what has worked for me and our family. It's what I believe in my heart of hearts that's given me direction, clarity, and drive. When we know whose we are, it's then that we figure out who we are.

ABOUT THE AUTHORS

Latricia Robinson-Dancer
My Life Restored
317-864-3838
Myliferestored7@gmail.com

Ron Fudge
The Original Strategist
269-861-1177
ronfudge7@gmail.com

Monica Sanders-Gates
God Said Live!
574-904-7031
designsbymomo@gmail.com

Kristy Jones
Called to Love
krjones215@gmail.com

Cassemdreia "Missy" O'Neal
Journey
317-410-6079
Missylondon@icloud.com

Choyce Guice-Robertson, LPN, Coach, Consultant
Knowledge Is Power
317-993-4065
cguicerobertson@gmail.com

Jarvay Robertson
Finding Me
Finding1me@gmail.com

Tiauna Ross
A Road in the Wilderness
info@tiaunaross.com
www.tiaunaross.com

Sabrinna Stennette
Change Me
Sabrinnastennette@gmail.com

Karenina Terry
Let It Go
317-626-4607
Terrykarenina@gmail.com

Stacia D. Washington
"When God is Positioning You…Follow Directions"
(317) 809-0908
thevirtuouswoman247@gmail.com

LaTasha White
From Here to There
765-252-GROW
givin2016@gmail.com
johncmaxwellgroup.com/latashawhite

AUTHENTIC IDENTITY INSTITUTE

LIST OF SERVICES

COACHING

One on One

Group

KEYNOTE TALKS

Live Out Loud (ROAR)

SIGNificance

The Power of Authenticity

CERTIFICATIONS

5D Coaching Certification

Human Behavior Consultant Certification

SEMINARS

5D Authentically ME™

5D Authentic Men

5D Authentic Identi-Teen

5D Authentically Me & You Couples Course

Authentically Me-Bully Free

ASSESSMENTS

(DISC) Personality Assessment

Spiritual Gift Assessment

JOHN MAXWELL CURRICULUM

Leadership Training

Mastermind Groups

Speaking

AIC BOOK PUBLISHING PARTNERSHIP DIVISION

www.authenticinstitute.com

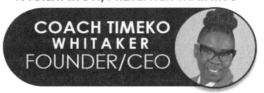

NOTES

NOTES

NOTES

NOTES

NOTES

NOTES

NOTES